SAS® 9 Study Guide

BICENTENNIAL
1807
WILEY
2007
BICENTENNIAL

THE WILEY BICENTENNIAL—KNOWLEDGE FOR GENERATIONS

*E*ach generation has its unique needs and aspirations. When Charles Wiley first opened his small printing shop in lower Manhattan in 1807, it was a generation of boundless potential searching for an identity. And we were there, helping to define a new American literary tradition. Over half a century later, in the midst of the Second Industrial Revolution, it was a generation focused on building the future. Once again, we were there, supplying the critical scientific, technical, and engineering knowledge that helped frame the world. Throughout the 20th Century, and into the new millennium, nations began to reach out beyond their own borders and a new international community was born. Wiley was there, expanding its operations around the world to enable a global exchange of ideas, opinions, and know-how.

For 200 years, Wiley has been an integral part of each generation's journey, enabling the flow of information and understanding necessary to meet their needs and fulfill their aspirations. Today, bold new technologies are changing the way we live and learn. Wiley will be there, providing you the must-have knowledge you need to imagine new worlds, new possibilities, and new opportunities.

Generations come and go, but you can always count on Wiley to provide you the knowledge you need, when and where you need it!

WILLIAM J. PESCE
PRESIDENT AND CHIEF EXECUTIVE OFFICER

PETER BOOTH WILEY
CHAIRMAN OF THE BOARD

SAS® 9 Study Guide

Preparing for the Base Programming Certification Exam for SAS® 9

Ali Hezaveh

WILEY-INTERSCIENCE
A John Wiley & Sons, Inc., Publication

To my wife, Mojgan

Contents

3 Managing Data

Index

Preface

The goal of this book is to help students understand the finepoints of Base SAS, and to help candidates pass the Base SAS certification exam. However, the material and the methods used in the text are also designed to allow SAS users to use the text as a quick reference for the SAS system. For each area under consideration, numerous examples, or short programs are provided.

On completion of this book, the reader should have a good understanding of the material and the concepts needed in order to write programs in Base SAS. I hope, with more than 15 years of experience in teaching and working with SAS, that I can make any part of this journey through SAS more effective or more enjoyable.

This book is intended for people who would like to take the Base SAS Programming certification exam, or for students who would like to use it as a companion text book in a major field, such as statistics or computer science. Candidates who want to take the Base SAS certification exam, students who want to learn SAS, or professionals who have forgotten some of the fine points of SAS can all benefit from this book.

This book assumes that the reader has an understanding of the keywords and statements that make a SAS program. For readers who have no background with SAS, I recommend the classic work, *SAS Programming by Example*, written by two pioneers in teaching SAS, Ron Cody and Ray Pass.

With the different versions of SAS, even the most knowledgeable programmer needs help in preparing for the exam. This book should shorten the preparation time for the Base SAS certification exam. Concepts, processes, and applications included in the exam are presented in a step-by-step format in the text as are short programs and tables with concise explanations. To enable the reader to achieve maximum benefit from the material, an assessment exam has been provided in the introduction.

I would like to thank the following colleagues from Georgia State University:
Dr. Kim King, Department of Computer science, for helping while the book was still in its early stage.; Margorie E. Hicks, Department of Mathematics and Statistics, for her thorough reading of all chapters and for making numerous corrections, excellent comments, and suggestions; Fred Brendel, Department of Mathematics and Statistics, for initially editing all chapters; and Dr. Subhashish Samaddar and Dr. Satish V. Nargundkar, Department of Managerial Sciences, for their help in reviewing the manuscript and for making useful suggestions to improve the text.
I would like to thank my colleague Dr. Jennifer Priestley of Kennesaw State University, Department of Mathematics for her insightful comments on the first two chapters of the book.
My sincere thanks go to the editor of the book, **Jacqueline Palmieri** , for her patience and her contributions. I am indebted to Steve Quigley at John Wiley for his persistent encouragement in the publishing of this text.

Introduction

Each chapter is divided into Topics, provided by the SAS Institute, to help candidates prepare for taking the exam. A brief explanation of each topic is given, followed by examples, and then tips. *Programs in this book are run on SAS® version 9.*

The chapter "Summaries" are concise reviews of the chapter material and a restatement of the main points.

At the end of each chapter a "two-minute drill" is provided as a checklist of the key points of the chapter; it can be used for last-minute review. The "assessment exam" offers questions that require short answers. The answers to the assessment exam questions follow the exam. Multiple-choice questions similar to those found on the exam are provided in the "practice exam". The answers to the practice exam questions, as well as explanations of these answers, are given at the end of the exam. Taking the practice exam after completing each chapter will reinforce what has been learned from that chapter. Candidates will also become familiar with the structure of the exam while taking the practice exam. To enable the candidate to practice, in depth, the material presented in the chapters, a set of problems followed by solutions are provided.

Sometimes a summary of what has been or is about to be studied is needed. Finally, tables similar to the one below, are given to summarize the material has been covered or will be covered.

Type of combination	Total number of observations in the output
Set a b;	Sum of observations in both datasets
Set a b; by name;	Total number of observations in both datasets
Set a ; Set b;	Number of observations in smallest dataset
Merge a b;	Number of observations in largest dataset
Merge a b; by name;	Total number of observations in each BY group in all datasets
Update a b; by name;	Sum of observations in master dataset and unmatched ones in transaction dataset

The Base SAS certification exam is the first of five certification tools the SAS Institute offers to track each candidates progress and is an industrywide-recognized program. The certification verifies competence in basic SAS programming. The exam covers generally assumed knowledge held by a SAS programmer. The SAS certification enjoys wide recognition in the computer industry and should help programmers secure and maintain employment

Passing the Base SAS certification exam creates an opportunity to increase earning potential, and demonstrates to employer that these programmers are keeping current with the latest development in the field. If SAS was learned through trial and error on-the-job rather than taking formal courses, passing the exam testifies that the SAS skills are credible.

Passing the multiple-choice computer-based exam certifies a candidate as a professional. There are no prerequisites, although the SAS Institute expects the candidates to have one year of SAS programming experience. There is no required training course, but the SAS Institute offers one for those who would like to take it. There is a fee for taking the exam, and candidates are notified immediately thereafter as to whether they passed it. A candidate who passes the exam becomes a SAS Certified Professional Programmer. There are no annual dues, and no further education is required in order to maintain the certification.

The exam is practical with little concern for theory. It consists of 70 multiple-choice questions; 46 questions must be answered correctly to pass. Each exam question falls into one of the five following topics, provided by SAS Institute:
1. Accessing data
2. Creating data structures
3. Managing data
4. Generating reports
5. Handling errors

These topics must be mastered to pass the certification exam. The maximum time allowed to complete the exam is two hours.

All questions in the SAS certification exam are in multiple-choice format, with either a single correct answer or multiple correct answers. When answering a question, a candidate may not know the number of correct answers! Candidates are often told explicitly how many correct answers there are.

Despite having many years of experience with SAS, it is possible that you may not have developed all the necessary understanding and skills needed to handle the SAS system. Although I had several years of experience with SAS, I did not realize how many finer points of the system that I had failed to master until I took the SAS certification exam for the first time. Realizing my shortcomings, I gathered a great deal of information and wrote small programs. I examined the output of these programs, made various changes, examined the kinds of error were propagated, and noted how the output changed after correcting each error.

This book is the outgrowth of the materials I collected for the exam and the programs I wrote and executed. After I passed the certification exam, I thought it would be a good idea to have a collection of the finer points of SAS available in one place.

The examination is administered at an authorized Prometric testing center. There are many Prometric testing centers across United States and Canada and in over 70 countries across the globe. You may take the exam at any testing center. All testing centers and their addresses are listed online on the Prometric Web page www.prometric.com . To register in the United States and Canada call 1-888-895-5819 or go to www.2test.com. Outside the United States and Canada, contact the Prometric regional service in your country. At the time of this writing, the cost to take the test was $150 (U.S.). The price is subject to change without notice, so always check the Prometric center Website(www.prometric.com) for current pricing. You must pay for the exam when you schedule it, so have your Social Security number (or international equivalent) and a credit card available. Prometric can bill you, but you will not be able to take the test until the payment is received in full. If you are unable to take the exam at the scheduled time, reschedule it at least one business day in advance; otherwise the fee will need to be repaid in full.

Any question or remarks concerning this book can be forwarded to the author by email.

Take the following assessment exam to evaluate your readiness to tackle the certification exam and determine those areas in which you need further work to strengthen your SAS skills.

1. In the SAS systems, what can the name of a variable begin with? What can it include?
2. Is SAS case-sensitive?
3. What does every statement end in?
4. What are the attributes of a variable?
5. What are the attributes of a SAS dataset?
6. What is an INPUT statement used for?
7. What is an INFILE statement used for?
8. What values can a numerical variable have?
9. What does it mean when we say " SAS statements are free format"?
10. When reading the raw data, what do you have to assign in the INPUT statement?
11. To list the information in a SAS dataset, which procedure should you use?
12. By default, what does PROC PRINT display?
13. What are the different ways to combine SAS datasets?
14. If you are combining SAS datasets using one SET statement, what is the total number of observations in the output dataset?
15. If you combine two SAS datasets (one called "master", the other called "transaction") using the UPDATE statement, how many observations will be included in the output dataset?
16. What are "line pointers"?
17. What are "column pointers"?

Carefully read over the explanation for any question you got wrong and note the chapter(s) in which material is presented. The assessment exam results are intended to help you plan a study strategy. Answers to the preceding questions are as follows:

1. A letter, or an underscore. They can include letters, numbers and underscores.
2. No.
3. Every statement ends in a semicolon.
4. There are six attributes: name, type, length, format or informat, position, label.
5. There are four attributes: name, date of creation, number of observations it includes, number of variables it contains.
6. INPUT is used to read raw data into SAS systems.

7. INFILE statement specifies the file containing the raw data.
8. Digits, +, -, ., E(for scientific representation of a number)
9. They can begin and end in any column; one statement can continue over several lines, or several statements can appear on the same line.
10. A valid SAS name, a type (character or numeric), a length.
11. PROC PRINT.
12. All observations and variables in the dataset, a column for observation numbers on the far left, variables in the order they occur in the dataset.
13. Concatenating, interleaving, one-to-one reading, one-to-one merging, match-merging, updating
14. The total number of observations in the output dataset is the sum of all observations in all data sets.
15. The sum of the largest number of observations in the master dataset and unmatched ones in the transaction dataset.
16. Line pointers will appear as # and /.
17. Column pointers will appear as @ and @@.

1   Accessing Data

Certification objectives

In this chapter you will learn what you need to pass this section of the exam:

- **Using formated, list, and column input to read raw data**
- **Using INFILE statement options**
- **Using various components of an INPUT statement**
- **Accessing existing SAS datasets**
- **Combining SAS datasets**

Welcome to the exciting world of creating SAS datasets. This first chapter will help you understand the basics of creating SAS datasets by focusing on INPUT and INFILE statements and their options. Along the way, we will see how to combine SAS datasets using DATA step statements. At the conclusion of the chapter you can test your level of understanding and retention of the material of this chapter by answering the questions in the "practice test" section. Answers to these questions are provided at the end of the section. A few problems with solutions have also been provided at the end of the chapter.

The SAS system can work only on SAS datasets. If the data you need are in raw form (i.e., a form other than SAS), then the first step is to transform the raw data into a SAS dataset. This is done in a DATA step. In the DATA step statement, you name the dataset that you are creating. The raw data are read into the dataset using an INPUT statement. If the raw data are in a file that is external to the environment where the SAS code is being written, then you refer to the raw data by an INFILE statement. The raw data can be entered instream at the same time SAS code is being written using a DATALINES statement or a CARDS statement.

Different forms of INPUT code are used to read raw data. In this chapter we discuss these forms and look at the INFILE statement and its options. We present sample programs and useful tips from the author that he used while preparing to take the SAS certification exam.

1.1 Using FORMATTED, LIST, and COLUMN input to read raw data files

The INPUT statement tells SAS how the raw data values are arranged and assigns input values to corresponding SAS variables. Each SAS variable can be read using one of the input systems: LIST, COLUMN, FORMATTED and NAMED input. SAS assumes that variables are numeric unless you designate that they are character. A character variable is created by placing a dollar sign ($) after the variable name separated by a blank.

There are four types of input statements. The style you select depends on the layout of the data values in the data records. You can combine different styles:

1. LIST input
2. COLUMN input
3. FORMATTED input
4. NAMED input

1.1.1 LIST input

Example 1.1
input name $ score1 score2;

Data values do not need to be aligned in columns but they must be separated by at least one blank or other delimiters such as a comma. As the name of the input implies, data must be in the form of a list. The first group of data values that SAS finds is assigned to the first variable on the INPUT statement, the next group to the next variable, and so on.

The default delimiter is one blank. A missing value must be shown with a period and not a blank. Data must be in standard numeric or character format.

For reading character values longer than 8, say, 12, the following line must be used *before* the INPUT statement:

Length name $12;

The SAS system cuts character variables at the first blank regardless of the length you have provided. Consequently they must not contain blanks. In the following example the character variable is longer than 8 bytes.

Example 1.2
```
data a;
input name $ code;
cards;
abcdefghijk 77
bob 404
;
run;
proc print data=a;
run;
```

Output:

```
        Obs     name       code
         1      abcdefgh     77
         2      bob         404
```

TIP: If you have a blank in a variable's value and use the length statement, SAS cuts it at the first blank it encounters and assumes that the remaining characters are for the next variable. In the next example the character variable exceeds 8 bytes and contains a blank space.

Example 1.3
```
data a ;
length name $13;
input name $ dob;
cards;
aabbccddee ff 123456
;
run;
proc print data=a;
run;
```

Output:

```
            Obs        name        dob
            1       aabbccddee       .
```

The following example shows that the numeric values can be longer than 8 bytes:

Example 1.4
```
data b;
input name $ dob;
cards;
aabbccddee 1234567890
;
run;
proc print data=b;
run;
```

Here is the output from Example 1.4:

```
            Obs        name           dob
            1       aabbccdd      1234567890
```

If there is a dash (–) in the zip values, SAS puts a period for `zip` in the output:

Example 1.5
```
data a;
input name $  state $ zip;
cards;
```

```
ali ga 30-3
;
run;
proc print data=a;
run;
```

Output:

Obs	name	state	zip
1	ali	ga	.

Wwithin the DATALINES, if there is a blank for a character or numeric variable, such as for `zip` in Example 1.6 SAS goes to the next value in the dataset, in this case to the next line and assumes this is the value for the variable. In example 1.6 `fan` is the next value and since it is a character value and *zip* is a numeric variable then it puts a period (.) for *zip* and inserts a note in the log saying: invalid data for *zip* on line ...

Example 1.6
```
data b;
input name $ state $ zip;
cards;
ali ga 303
jon nc
fan ny 404
;
run;
proc print data=b;
run;
```

Output:

Obs	name	state	zip
1	ali	ga	303
2	jon	nc	.

What happens if there is a period in the data for a character or numeric variable?

If in the datalines in place of ali there is a period, then the data value ali in the output, would be replaced with a blank. But if there is a period for *zip* (which is a numeric variable), it adds a period for `zip` in the output.

1.1.2 COLUMN input

Example 1.7
input name $ 1 – 12 score 17 – 20;

    Columns of data must be aligned. After each variable name you must specify a column position. If a variable is a character, then a dollar sign ($) would precede the column designation. Data must be in standard numeric or character form. Total number of character values can range from 1 to 200 characters long.
    No placeholder, such as a single period, is required for missing data.
    Values need not be separated by blanks or other delimiters. Input values can be read in any order, regardless of their position in the record. Character values can have embedded blanks. Variables and parts of variables can be read in any order.

TIP: If there is a blank in the value of a numeric variable, SAS gives an error in the log and it places a period for the value of that variable in the outpu.

In the following example, note the space between 12 and 13 , value of `score` is supposed to be 1213:

Example 1.8
```
Data a;
Input name $ 1 - 3 score 5 - 10;
Cards;
Ali 12 13
run;
proc print data=a;
run;
(notice)
```

Output:

Obs	name	score
1	Ali	.

    The message in the log is `error`=1 invalid data for score in line 4. But if there is a blank in the value of a character variable (here `name`), no error will result.

Example 1.9
```
Data u;
Input name $ 1-4 score;
Cards;
A li 1213
;
run;
```

```
proc print data=u;
run;
```

Output:

```
                        Obs    name    score
                        1      A li    1213
```

1.1.3 FORMATTED input

```
Input name $12.  +4  score1 comma5.  +6  score comma5. ;
```

The formatted input enables you to read *nonstandard* data. It is typically used with pointer controls that determine over the position of the input pointer in the input buffer when reading data(i.e. it allows you to indicate the beginning column of a variable and then specify the length of the variable). The last input statement uses formatted input and pointer controls. Note that $12. and comma5. are informats, whereas +4 and +6 are column pointer controls.

Character values can contain embedded blanks. Character values can range from 1 to 200 in number.

No placeholder such as a single period is required for a missing data value.

Values or parts of values can be reread. Input values can be read in any order.

TIP: With comma5. *as the format for a numeric value, it is fine if you have a blank in the data.*

Example 1.10
```
Data h;
Input name $3.  +2 score comma5. ;
Cards;
Abc  22 33
;
run;
```

Output:

```
                        Obs    name    score
                        1      Abc     2233
```

If you do not have commaw. as the format and there is a blank in the numeric data, SAS gives an error message in the log and a period as its value in the output (see Example 1.8).

1.1.4 NAMED input

```
Input name=bob code=404;
```

NAMED input is used to read records in which data values are preceded by the name of the variable and an equal sign. When in an INPUT statement, an equal sign follows a variable, the SAS system expects that data remaining on the input line to contain only named input values. After using NAMED input, you can*not* switch to another form of input in the same input statement.

Example 1.11

```
data a;
input name=$ salary= tax=;
cards;
name=ghb salary=100 tax=8
;
run;
proc print data=a;
run;
```

Output:

```
The SAS System                12:22 Monday, May 30, 2005    1
                         Obs       name       salary       tax
                         1         ghb          100         8
```

1.2 Using INFILE statement options to control processing when reading raw data files

An INFILE statement identifies an external file of raw data that you are trying to read with an INPUT statement. An INFILE statement must be executed before an INPUT statement. You can use INFILE in conditional processing, for example, with an IF-THEN statement.

In one DATA step you can use many INFILE and INPUT statements.
To use the INFILE statement, the dataset has to be a *raw* dataset, not a SAS dataset.

Example 1.12

```
Data b;
Infile 'c:\mydata\a.txt' firstobs=2;
```

(The data set a is created by using Microsoft Word and saved as text in the file mydata in c directory.) The option firstobs=2 is used because the first line of data in the data file is the name of the variables, not a data value.

If you want to read the entire dataset, use the INFILE statement without any option. If you need to read part of your raw data, use INFILE statement options *firstobs* = n , *obs* = m (n is observation number where you begin reading data, and m is the place where you finish it).

To deal with other circumstances of raw data files, the INFILE statement has 34 options to help you; three such options are: (1) MISSOVER, (2) PAD, and (3) TRUNCOVER.

1.2.1 MISSOVER

When used in an INFILE statement, the INPUT statement does not jump to the next line when reading a short line; instead it sets the value of the variable to "missing".

In the next example the raw data contain three variables. The values of score, age or both are missing for some objects.

Example 1.13
```
data aa;
infile datalines ;
input name $ age score;
datalines;
jones 67 88
noles 34
rather
walters 45 89
;
run;
proc print data=aa;
run;
```

Output (note that the third row of data has disappeared):

Obs	name	age	score
1	jones	67	88
2	noles	34	.
3	walters	45	89

Now, let's use the option MISSOVER and look at the output:
```
data aa;
infile datalines missover;
input name $ age score;
datalines;
jones 67 88
noles 34
rather
```

```
walters 45 89
;
run;
proc print data=aa;
run;
```

Output, using MISSOVER:

```
            Obs      name        age      score
            1        jones       67       88
            2        noles       34       .
            3        rather      .        .
            4        walters     45       89
```

1.2.2 PAD

The PAD option adds blanks to the lines to fill or "Flesh" them out to the logical length. This is why it works correctly and completely with column input.

   Note that the data in the following DAATA STEP are short on line 2 (same data values are used as in Example 1.13). SAS goes to the next line and brings the value of id and ignores the rest of the line, (data were created with Microsoft Word and saved as "text only" on a floppy disk).

Example 1.14
```
libname ab 'a:\';
data ab.oo;
filename abc 'a:\mine.txt';
infile abc ;
input id 1-3 age 5-6 hrly 8-10 wgt 12-14 hgt 16-18;
run;
proc print data=ab.oo;
run;
```

Output:

```
       Obs   id   age   hrly   wgt    hgt
       1     1    56    64     130    80
       2     2    44    72     180    3
```

   Now, let's use the PAD option of the INFILE statement and pay attention to the output. The output is complete and the third line has all its values in place. On line 2 there is a missing value for the variable hgt (height).

```
libname ab 'a:\';
data ab.oo;
filename abc 'a:\mine.txt';
infile abc pad;
input id 1-3 age 5-6 hrly 8-10 wgt 12-14 hgt 16-18;
run;
proc print data=ab.oo;
run;
```

Output, using option PAD:

Obs	id	age	hrly	wgt	hgt
1	1	56	64	130	80
2	2	44	72	180	.
3	3	64	78	140	88

1.2.3 TRUNCOVER

TRUNCOVER is similar to MISSOVER, but it accepts partial values as well. If the length of a variable is declared to be 9 in the INPUT statement but a data value has a length of 6, the 6 length value is accepted.

More specifically, if we have *name* $ 1 - 9, but the data value is ali, thus it accepts ali as the value for that variable.

In summary; MISSOVER gives best results with list input. TRUNCOVER gives best results with column and list input. PAD works best with column input.

1.3 Using various components of an INPUT statement

To use the starting column of a data and the length of data value, you can use column pointer @. If a set of data for an observation exceeds a few lines on the raw data, you can tell SAS which line contains the next data value by using a line pointer # or /.

Column and line pointers are provided in the INPUT statement to enable you to reset the pointer's column and line position when telling the INPUT statement where to read the data value in the data record.

1.3.1 Column pointer

Column pointers are indicated by the symbols @ and @@. When @ and @@, are used they must appear at the *end* of an INPUT statement.

Trailing @ holds an input record for the execution of the next input statement.

Double trailing @ holds the input record for the execution of the next input statement, even across iterations of the DATA step.

Single @ applies for more complex situation(s) while the double trailing @ keeps the raw data line until nothing is left to read.

Example 1.15
```
Data a;
Input x y @@;
Cards;
1 2 3 4
;
run;
proc print data=a;
run;
```

Output:

Obs	x	y
1	1	2
2	3	4

If you put one @ or nothing it reads the value of 1 only for x and 2 for y.
Let's look at an example for one trailing @ at the end of the INPUT statement:

Example 1.16
```
Data m;
Input @ 15 type $1. @;
If type = 1 then input id 1 - 3 age 4 - 5 weight 6 - 8;
Else if type = 2 then input id 1 - 3 age 10 - 11 weight 15 -
17;
Cards;
00134168
00245155        1
003    23 220 2
;
run;
proc print data=m;
run;
```

Output:

Obs	type	id	age	weight
1	1	2	45	155
2	2	3	2	2

Two different types of data are necessary because the sources of the data vary. The data are the same but are at different positions depending on source. There is an identifying value in each observation (e.e, as in `type` in Example 1.16) that denotes the source of data.

1.3.2 Line pointer

Line pointers are denoted by the symbols # and /. If a set of data for an observation spans multiple lines (records) on the raw data file, we use line pointers # or /. The following dataset has two lines of data for each `id` and the program uses #:

Example 1.17
```
Data b;
Input #1 @1 id 3. @5 gender $1. @7 age 2.
      #2 @5 weight 3. @9 age 3. @13 height 3.;
datalines;
100 m 26 68 012366
100 120  80 68
200 m 32 78 031460
200 162  92 72
;
proc print data=b;
run;
```

Output:

Obs	id	gender	age	weight	height
1	100	m	80	120	68
2	200	m	92	162	72

This program states that at line 1 of the raw data, `id` begins at column 1 and is three characters long, `gender` begins at column 5, and so on. Also, at line 2, `weight` begins at column 5 and is three character long.

Suppose that you have a file of raw data with four records per observation, and you want to read only three variables (*id*, *name*, *salary*) from the second record. This is how it's done:

```
Input #2 id $1. name $ 5. salary #4;
```

Notice that you are not reading anything from record 4, but you have to mention #4 so SAS recognizes that each observation has four records.

Using slash(/)

Use multiple slashes to skip unwanted records of raw data and bring in the ones you want. If you want to go to the next line of raw data for each observation, this is how to do it:

```
Input @1 id 3. @5 gender $1. @7 age 2.
        /  @5 name 3. @9 lname 3. @ 13 hoby 3.;
```

One slash sends the pointer to the next line, two slashes to two lines down, and so on.

Combining / and

You can combine the two methods. For example, if each record of raw data has four lines, then we have

```
Input #2 id $1. name $ 5. salary //;
```

This is equivalent to

```
Input #2 id $1. name $ 5. salary #4;
```

TIP: At the end of your exam period it is better if you guess some of the questions rather than leaving them blank.

1.4 Accessing existing SAS datasets with DATA step statements

Use POINT = variable to read SAS datasets using random (direct) access by observation number. With POINT = option, a temporary variable is created whose value is the number of the observation you want the SET statement to read. This variable is not added to any new SAS dataset. The POINT= variable is available anywhere in the DATA step. The POINT= variable must always be used in a DO loop, or as an index. The POINT = option reads from the observation it starts with to the end of the dataset. It can*not* be used with a BY or a WHERE statement or an SQL(structured query language) procedure.

Example 1.18
```
Data a;
Do i=1 to 4;
Set aa.bb point = i;
Output;
End;
Stop;
run;
```

When you use the POINT = option, you must also include in your program a STOP statement; otherwise you get an infinite loop. If in the SET statement the `i` is replaced with 2, an error in the log will be saying: "expecting a name".

TIP: Before answering the trickier questions, read the exam over completely; sometimes information supplied in later questions gives some hint for earlier ones.

1.5 Combining SAS datasets using DATA step statements

In this section we look at different ways to create a new SAS dataset from existing ones. Any new SAS dataset can be a subset of an old one, a combination of a few existing ones, or an update of an existing SAS dataset.

To accomplish these tasks one, can use different methods and different SAS statements. The SQL (structured query language) of the SAS systems also provides a whole new methodology for combining data sets. For many situations old tools such as SET and MERGE are easier and preferred methods.

In the DATA STEP you can use SET, MERGE, or UPDATE statements to combine SAS datasets in one of the following six ways:
1. Concatenating
2. Interleaving
3. One-to-one reading
4. One-to-one merging
5. Match-merging
6. Updating

Summary of different methods used to combine SAS datasets where (a and b are SAS data sets):

Type of combination	Total noumber of observations in output
Set a b;	Total number of observations in both datasets
Set a b;	Total number of observations in both datasets
By name;	
Set a;	Number of observations in smallest dataset
Set b;	
Merge a b;	Number of observations in largest dataset
Merge a b;	total argest number of observations each
By name;	BY group in all datasets
Update master transact;	Sum of observations in master dataset and unmatched
By name;	ones in transaction dataset

If the length of a variable is different in different data sets , SAS takes the length from the First dataset.

Format, informat, label, length (if they are not explicitly defined) of the First dataset overrides other datasets'.

If you are using BY processing to combine datasets, make sure that each data set is sorted by the BY variable.

1.5.1 Concatenating

Concatenating is the combination of two or more datasets one after the other(consecutively) in a single dataset. The number of observations in the new data set is the sum of the number of observations in the original datasets. The order is all observations from the first dataset followed by those from the second dataset and so on.

Example 1.19
```
Data a;
Set b c d;
run;
```

1.5.2 Interleaving

Interleaving involves the use of a SET statement and a BY statement to combine datasets into a new dataset. You can assume a SET statement to be similar to an INPUT statement with the difference that the SET statement reads lines of data from a SAS dataset while an INPUT statement reads *raw* lines of data from an instream data or an external file. The number of observations in the new dataset is the sum of the number of observations from the original datasets. The observations in the new dataset are arranged by the values of the BY variable and, within each BY group, by the order of the datasets in which they occur.

Before you can interleave data sets, the observations must be sorted by the variable used in the BY statement.

DATA STEP processing during interleaving involves three steps:
1. The descriptor of each dataset is read into the program data vector. The SAS system also creates FIRST.variable and LAST.variable for each variable listed in the BY statement.
2. The SAS system compares the first observation from each dataset to determine which BY group should appear first in the new dataset. It reads all observations from the first BY group from the selected dataset. If this BY group appears in more than one dataset, it reads from the datasets in the order in which they appear in the SET statement. The values of the variables in the program data vector are set to "missing" each time the SAS system starts to read a new dataset and when the BY group changes.
3. The SAS system compares the next available observation from each dataset to determine the next BY group and starts reading observations from selected datasets in the SET statement that contains observations for this BY group. The SAS system continues in this manner until it has read all observations from all datasets.

Example 1.20
```
Data a;
Input type $ animal $;
Cards;
a ant
a ape
b bird
c cat
;
run;

data b;
input type $ tree $;
cards;
```

```
a apple
b banana
c coconut
;
run;
data c;
set a b;
by type;
run;
Output:
```

```
Obs      type      animal      tree
1        a         ant
2        a         ape
3        a                     apple
4        b         bird
5        b                     banana
6        c         cat
7        c                     coconut
```

TIP: If one of the variables is numeric and has no value on some lines of data, then in the output there will appear a period when interleaving the dat sets:

Example 1.21
```
Data a;
Input type $ animal $ salary;
Cards;
a ant 100
a ape .
b bird 200
c cat .
;
run;
data c;
set a b;
by type;
run;
proc print data=c;
run;
Output:
```

```
Obs      type      animal      salary      tree
1        a         ant         100
2        a         ape         .
3        a                     .           apple
4        b         bird        200
5        b                     .           banana
6        c         cat         .
7        c                     .           coconut
```

Notice the periods for the numeric variable `salary` and blanks for the character variables in the output dataset.

1.5.3 One-to-one reading

One-to-one reading combines observations from two or more datasets into one observation using two or more SET statements. The new dataset combines all variables from the input datasets. The number of observations in the dataset is the number of observations from the smallest original dataset. It stops reading from other datasets if they have more observations. If datasets contain common variables, the values read in from the last dataset replace those read in from earlier ones.

Example 1.22
```
Data a ;
Input type $ animal $;
Cards;
a ant
b bird
c cat
;
run;

data b;
input type $ tree $;
cards;
a apple
b banana
c coconut
;
run;

data c;
set a;
set b;
run;
proc print data=c;
run;
```

Output:

```
          Obs    type    animal      tree
          1       a       ant       apple
          2       b       bird      banana
          3       c       cat       coconut
```

Example 1.23
In the following example note that dataset b has one less record of data than does dataset a.
```
Data a;
Input type $ animal $;
Cards;
a ant
b bird
c cat
;
run;

data b;
input type $ tree $;
cards;
a apple
b banana
;
run;

data c;
set a;
set b;
run;
proc print data=c;
run;
```

Output:

Obs	type	animal	tree
1	a	ant	apple
2	b	bird	banana

1.5.4 One-to-one merging

One-to-one merging combines observations from one or more SAS datasets into a single observation in a new dataset.

Example 1.24
```
Data c;
Merge a b;
Run;
```
Data sets a and b are as in the previous example.

Obs	type	animal	tree
1	a	ant	apple
2	b	bird	banana
3	c	cat	coconut

The number of observations in the new dataset is equal to the number of observations in the largest dataset.

DATA STEP processing during one-to-one merging is as follows:

1. A data vector is created that contains all variables from all datasets.

2. SAS reads the first observation from each dataset, in the same order that they appear in the MERGE statement. If two datasets contain the same variables, the values from the second dataset replace those from the first.

3. Steps 1 and 2 continue until all observations from all datasets are read.

1.5.5 Match-Merging

Match-merging combines observations from two or more SAS datasets into a single observation in a new dataset according to the values of a common variable. The number of observations in the new dataset is the sum of the(i.e. , total) largest number of observations in each BY group in all datasets. All datasets must be sorted by the variable specified in the BY group.

Example 1.25
```
Data a;
Input type $ animal $;
Cards;
a ant
b bird
c cat
;
run;

data b;
input type $ tree $;
cards;
a apple
b banana
c coco
;
run;

data c;
merge a b;
by type;
```

```
run;
proc print data=c;
run;
```

Output:

Obs	type	animal	tree
1	a	ant	apple
2	b	bird	banana
3	c	cat	coco

Data processing during match-merging proceeds as follows:
1. SAS creates a program data vector that contains all the variables from all datasets.
2. SAS looks at the first BY group in each dataset named in the merge statement to determine which BY group should appear first in the dataset.
3. The first observation in that BY group from each dataset is read. If a dataset does not have an observation in that BY group, the program data vector will contain missing values for the variable unique to that dataset.

Duplicate values of the BY variable

When the last observation from a BY group in one dataset has been read into the program data vector, the SAS system retains its values for all variables unique to that dataset until all observations for that BY group have been read from all datasets.

Example 1.26
```
Data a;
Input type $ animal $;
datalines;
a ant
a ape
b bird
c cat
;
run;

data b;
input type $ tree $;
cards;
a apple
b banana
c coco
c celery
;
run;
```

```
data c;
merge a b;
by type;
run;
proc print data=c;
run;
```

Output:

```
          Obs     type     animal      tree
           1       a         ant       apple
           2       a         ape       apple
           3       b         bird      banana
           4       c         cat       coco
           5       c         cat       celery
```

Nonmatched observations

The SAS system retains the values of all variables in the program data vector even if the value is missing. The following two programs do not contain all values of the BY variable type.

Example 1.27
```
Data a;
Input type $ animal $;
Cards;
a ant
c cat
d dog
e eagle
;
run;

data b;
input type $ tree $;
datalines;
a apple
b banana
c coco
e eggplant
f fig
;
run;

Data c;
```

```
Merge a b;
By type;
Run;
proc print data=c;
run;
```

Output:

```
Obs    type    animal     tree
1      a       ant        apple
2      b                  banana
3      c       cat        coco
4      d       dog
5      e       eagle      eggplant
6      f                  fig
```

The observations in the output dataset contain missing values for the variables that are in one dataset but not in the other.

1.5.6 Updating datasets

To update datasets, two datasets must be utilized. The dataset containing the original information is the master dataset, and the dataset containing the new information is the transaction dataset. You must use a BY statement with the UPDATE statement.

The number of observations in the new dataset is the sum of the number of observations in the master dataset and unmatched observations in the transaction dataset.

Example 1.28
```
data master;
input type $ animal $ tree $;
Cards;
a ant apple
b bird banana
;
run;

data transact;
input type $ tree $;
datalines;
a apricot
b barley
c coco
;
run;

data c;
merge master transact;
```

```
by type;
run;
proc print data=c;
run;
```

Output:

obs	type	animal	tree
1	a	ant	apricot
2	b	bird	barley
3	c		coco

In the next example notice how the missing values of the variables *salary* and *sex* affect the output.

Example 1.29
```
Data a;
Input name $ salary;
Cards;
ali 23
dave 66
;
run;

data b;
input name $ sex $;
cards;
bob 55 m
james 44 m
karl 22
;
run;

data c;
update a b;
by name;
run;
proc print data=c;
run;
```

Output:

Obs	name	salary	sex
1	ali	23	
2	bob	.	55
3	dave	66	
4	james	.	44
5	karl	.	22

DATA STEP processing to update datasets proceeds in the following order:
1. SAS creates a program data vector as well as FIRST.variable and LAST.variable for each variable in the BY statement.
2. SAS looks at the first observation in each dataset. If the transaction BY value precedes the master BY value, the SAS system reads from the transaction dataset only and sets the variable from the master data set to "missing". If the master BY value precedes the transaction BY value, SAS reads from the master dataset only and sets the variable from transaction dataset to "missing".
3. After completing the first transaction, the SAS system looks at the next observation in the transaction dataset. If it finds one with the same BY value, it applies that transaction as well. The first observation then contains the new values from both transactions.
4. If no other transactions exist for that observation, SAS writes the observation to the new dataset and sets the values in the program data vector to "missing".
5. SAS repeats these steps until all observations from all BY groups in both datasets have been read.

Chapter summary

This chapter demonstrated that the INPUT statement is the SAS system's main engine for creating SAS datasets from raw data existing in a wide variety of formats. Chapter 1 described that the INFILE statement can be used to read raw data. Some of the finer points of the components of the INPUT statement including line and column pointers and single and double trailing @ were considered. The procedure for accessing a SAS dataset randomly by observation number using the POINT = option was discussed. Different forms of combining SAS datasets for various cases were demonstrated.

Two-minute drill

- Data are read into a dataset using an INPUT statement.
- There are four different forms of an INPUT statement: FORMATTED, LIST, COLUMN, and NAMED.
- SAS assumes that variables are numeric unless you designate that they are character.
- A length statement must appear before an INPUT statement.
- In the LIST input, the default delimiter is one blank.
- In the LIST input statement, missing values must be denoted by a period.
- In the LIST or COLUMN input, numeric or character data must be in standard format.
- FORMATTED input enables you to read nonstandard data.
- The INFILE statement must be used for raw data set.
- Three important INFILE statement options are MISSOVER, TRUNCOVER and PAD.
- Trailing @ and double trailing @ appear at the end of an input statement.
- Line pointers are denoted # and /.
- To access a SAS dataset randomly by observation number, use the POINT = option.
- There are five different ways to combine SAS datasets using SET, MERGE, and UPDATE statements: concatenating, interleaving, one-to-one reading, one-to-one merging, match-merging, and updating.
- If you use one SET statement to combine datasets, the number of observations in the output dataset is the sum of observations in all the datasets (with or without the BY statement).
- If you use two SET statements to combine SAS datasets, the number of observations in the output data is the number of observations in the smallest dataset.
- If you use MERGE statement (without the BY statement), the number of observations in the output dataset is the number of observations in the largest dataset.

Assessment exam

Take the following assessment test to evaluate your readiness to tackle the certification exam.

1. In the SAS systems, with what can a variable begin? What can it include?
2. Is SAS case-sensitive?
3. What does every SAS statement end in?
4. What are the attributes of a variable?
5. What are the attributes of a SAS dataset?
6. What is the INPUT statement used for?
7. What is the INFILE statement used for?
8. What can a numerical variable contain?
9. What does it mean when we say '"SAS statements are free-format"?
10. When reading the raw data, what do you have to assign in the INPUT statement?
11. To list the information in a SAS dataset, which procedure do you use?
12. By default, what does PROC PRINT display?
13. What are the different ways to combine SAS datasets?
14. If you are combining SAS datasets using one SET statement, what is the total number of observations in the output dataset?
15. If you combine two SAS datasets (one called "master", the other called "transaction") using an UPDATE statement, how many observations will be in the output dataset?
16. What symbols denote line pointers?
17. What symbols denote column pointers?

Assessment exam answers

1. A letter or an underscore. They can include letters, numbers, and underscores.
2. No.
3. Every statement ends in a semicolon.
4. There are six attributes: name, type, length, format or informat, position, label.
5. There are four attributes: name, date on which the dataset was created, the number of observations in the dataset, and the number of variables the dataset has.
6. It is used to read raw data into SAS systems.
7. The INFILE statement specifies the file containing the raw data.
8. Digits, +, -, ., E(for scientific representation of a number).
9. SAS statements can begin and end in any column, or one statement can continue over several lines, or several statements can appear on the same line.
10. A valid SAS variable name, a type (character or numeric), and a length.
11. PROC PRINT.

12. All observations and variables in the dataset, with a column for observation numbers on the far left and variables in the order in which they occur in the dataset.
13. Concatenating, interleaving, one-to-one reading, one-to-one merging, match-merging, updating.
14. The total number of observations in the output dataset is the sum of all observations in all datasets.
15. The sum of the largest number of observations in the master dataset and unmatched ones in the transaction dataset.
16. The symbols # and /.
17. The symbols @ and @@.

Practice exam

The following questions are designed to help you measure the level of your understanding of the material presented in this chapter. Some questions may have more than one correct answer, so be careful when answering each question.

1. If you declare Social Security number (*ss#*) as a numeric variable in your list INPUT statement, and in the raw data (say, DATALINES) there is a dash in the value of ss#, what is the result in the output once you execute the DATA STEP?
   A. The ss# is printed in its complete form, including the dashes.
   B. SAS cuts the value of ss# at the first dash.
   C. SAS puts a period for ss# in the output.
   D. It eliminates the dash in the output and writes the nine digit value.

2. In LIST input if, *name* is declared to be a character variable, and in the raw data there is a period for *name*, what will be the value of *name* in the output once you execute the DATA STEP?
   A. You will get a period.
   B. There will be a blank.
   C. SAS brings in the value of the next variable and considers that value to belong to the variable *name*.
   D. There will be no output for the entire dataset.

3. In LIST input, if in the raw data (say, DATALINES) there is a blank for a character or numeric variable, and you execute the DATA STEP, what will be the result in the output?
   A. SAS will assigns the next value to the variable.
   B. SAS will leave a blank in the output.
   C. There will be no output for the entire dataset.
   D. SAS will insert a period for the value of the character variable or a blank for the numeric variable.

4. In COLUMN input, which one of the following is correct?
   A. A period is needed as a placeholder.
   B. A space is needed as a placeholder.
   C. No placeholder is needed.
   D. A period for a character variable or a blank for a numeric variable will be needed.

5. In the column INPUT, if there is a blank in the value of a numeric variable in the raw data, what will be the result once the DATA STEP is executed?
   A. SAS inserts a period in the output for the value of that variable.
   B. SAS will give an error message in the log.
   C. Includes the blank in the output for the value of that variable.
   D. Both A and B (above) will take place.

6. In COLUMN input, if there is a blank in the value of a character variable, what is the result in the output for the value of that variable once the DATA STEP is executed?
   A. A blank appears in the output and an error message is written in the log.
   B. A blank appears in the output but no error message is written in the log.
   C. SAS eliminates the blank in the output and writes the value of the variable without the blank.
   D. SAS inserts a period for the value of that variable.

7. In the given input statement `Input   name   $12. +4    grade1    comma5. +6 grade2 comma5.  ;` which one of the following is the column pointer?
   A. The period after the numbers 12 and 5
   B. The plus sign before the numbers 4 and 6
   C. Both A and B
   D. +4 and +6

8. In the FORMATTED input statement, which one of the following is correct?
   A. No placeholder is needed.
   B. Character values can contain blanks.
   C. Character values can not contain blanks.
   D. Values or a portion of a value can be read.
   E. A, C, and D are correct.
   F. A, B, and D are correct.
   G. A and B are correct.

9. In a DATA STEP, which statement(s) can be used?
   A. One INFILE and one INPUT statement
   B. One INFILE statement and many INPUT statements
   C. One INPUT statement and many INFILE statements
   D. Many INFILE and INPUT statements

10. To use an INFILE statement, the dataset must be:
    A. A SAS dataset
    B. A raw dataset
    C. A SAS or a raw dataset
    D. None of the above

11. When using the MISSOVER option in an INFILE statement, which one of the following actions takes place while reading a short line of data?
    A. The INPUT statement jumps to the next line.
    B. The INPUT statement does not jump to the next line.
    C. SAS sets the value of the variable to "missing".
    D. Both A and C.
    E. Both B and C.

12. Which of the following INFILE options add blanks to the lines of data to fill them out to the logical length?
    A. TRUNCOVER
    B. MISSOVER
    C. PAD
    D. All of the above

13. Which of the following give(s) the best result with list INPUT?
    A. MISSOVER
    B. TRUNCOVER
    C. Both A abd B
    D. PAD

14. PAD works best with which of the following input statements?
    A. LIST input
    B. COLUMN input
    C. FORMATTED input
    D. A and C
    E. B and C

15. Which of the following holds the input record for the execution of the next input statement?
    A. @
    B. ;
    C. /
    D. :

16. What is the default delimiter in the LIST input statement?
    A. One slash (/)
    B. One dash (–)
    C. One blank
    D. One period (.)

17. In theLIST input statement, a missing value must be shown with which of the following?
    A. A blank
    B. A period
    C. A dash (-)
    D. A slash (/)

18. Given the following DATA step
    ```
    Data a;
    Input a b @@;
    Cards;
    8 9 7 6
    q ;
    r  q     qun;
    ```
    after execution, which of the following is the dataset output?

```
A.  a       b
    8       9
    7       6
B.  a       b
    8       7
    9       6
C.  a       b
    8       9
D.  a       b
    .       9
    .       6
```

19. Which of the following is a line pointer?
    A. #
    B. /
    C. Both of the above
    D. None of the above

20. Suppose that you have a file of raw data with four records per observation and you want to read only two variables (*id, name*) from row 2, which of the following input statement does the job?
    A. Input #2 id $1. name $5. #3 ;
    B. Input #2 id $1. name $4. / ;
    C. Input #2 id name $5. /// ;
    D. Input #2 id $2. name $6. #4 ;

21. Which one of the following is true for POINT= option?
    A. It must not be used in a DO loop.
    B. It can be used with a BY or a WHERE statement.
    C. It reads from the observation it starts with to the end of dataset.
    D. It must be used in a loop but never as an index.

22. If you run the following DATA step
```
Data a;
 Do I=1 to 5;
 Set b point=I;
 Output;
 End;
 Run;
```
    which of the following describes the result of the execution?
    A. Data set a will have four observations.
    B. Data set a will have one observation.
    C. An infinite loop
    E. An error message saying "expecting a variable name".

23. If you run the following DATA step
    ```
    Data a;
    Do I=2 to 10;
    Set b point=3;
    Stop;
    End;
    Run;
    ```
    which of the following describes the result of the execution?
    A. An infinite loop
    B. An error message saying "expecting a name."
    C. Data set a will have seven observations
    D. Data set a will have one observation

24. Given the following DATA STEP:
    ```
    Data a;
    Set b;
    Set c;
    Run;
    ```
    how many observations will data set a have?
    A. Total number of observations in datasets b and c
    B. Number of observations in the largest dataset
    C. Number of observations in the smallest dataset
    D. Total number of observations in data set b and unmatched ones in dataset c

25. Given the following DATA STEP
    ```
    Data a;
    Merge b c;
    By name;
    Run;
    ```
    how many observations will dataset a have?
    A. Total number of observations in the master data set and unmatched ones in
        transaction data set
    B. Total largest number of observations in each BY group in all datasets
    C. Total number of observations in dataset a and dataset b
    D. Number of observations in the largest data set

26. Given the following data step:
    ```
    Data a;
    Update b c;
    By name;
    Run;
    ```
    How many observations will dataset a have?
    A. Total number of observations in b (master data set) and unmatched ones in c
        (transaction data set)
    B. Total largest number of observations in each BY group in all datasets
    C. Total number of observations in datasets a and b
    D. Number of observations in the largest dataset

27. Given the following DATA step
```
Data a;
Set  b c;
By name;
Run;
```
How many observations will data set a have?
A. Number of observations in the smallest dataset
B. Number of observations in the largest dataset
C. Total number of observations in both datasets
D. None of the above

28. When combining different datasets, SAS takes the length of a variable from
A. Last dataset.
B. First dataset.
C. Either A or B.
D. It ignores either A and B, and each time it sees the variable, it sets a new length for it

29. In the DATA step, when using SET, MERGE, and UPDATE statements, which one of the following is *not* a method for combining datasets?
A. One-to-one reading
B. Interleaving
C. Many-to-many reading
D. Match-merging

30. In the DATA step, when using SET, MERGE, and UPDATE statements, which one of the following is a method for combining datasets?
A. One-to-many reading
B. Many-to-one merging
C. One-to-one updating
D. Concatenating

31. Which one of the following is correct?
A. Informat, format, and label of the first dataset overrides the others
B. Informat, format, and label of the last dataset overrides the others
C. SAS decides for informat, format, and label of each data set as it encounters it.
D. None of the above

32. In the following DATA step
```
Data a;
Set b c d;
Run;
```
what is the order of the observation in dataset a?
A. All observations from dataset d, then all observations from c, next all observations from dataset a
B. All observations from dataset b, then all observations from c, next all observations from dataset d
C. All observations from smallest dataset only
D. All observations from largest dataset only

33. Given datasets aa and bb as follows:

```
data aa;
input name $ job $;
cards;
ali teacher
ali janitor
carol manager
dave ceo
;
run;

data bb ;
input name $ drink $;
cards;
ali milk
carol water
dave juice
;
run;
```

Dataset cc is created as follows:

```
data cc;
set aa bb;
by name;
run;
```

Which of the following is the content of dataset c?

	A. name	job	drink
	ali	teacher	
	ali	janitor	
	ali		milk
	carol	manager	
	carol		water
	dave	ceo	
	dave		juice
	B. name	job	drink
	ali	teacher	janitor
	ali	janitor	milk
	carol	manager	water
	dave	ceo	juice
	C. name	job	drink
	ali	teacher	janitor
	ali		milk
	carol	manager	water
	dave	ceo	juice
	D. name	job	drink
	ali	teacher	.
	ali	jaintor	

```
ali          .              milk
carol     manager
carol        .              water
dave      ceo                 .
dave         .              juice
```

34. Given datasets a and b as follows:

```
Data a;
Input com $ animal $ salary;
Cards;
a ant 100
a ape .
b bird 200
c cat .
;
run;

data b;
input com $ plant $;
cards;
b banana
c coconut
;
run;
```

Data set c is created as follows:

```
data c;
set a b;
by com;
run;
```

Which of the following is the content of dataset c?

```
A. com      animal      salary    plant
   a         ant          100
   a         ape           .
   b         bird         200
   b                       .        banana
   c         cat           .
   c                       .        coconut


B. com      animal      salary    plant
   a         ant          100
   a         ape                     .
   b         bird         200
   b                                banana
   c         cat                      .
   c                                coconut
C. com      animal      salary    plant
   a         ant          100
   a         ape
```

```
        b       bird      200
        b                           banana
        c       cat
        c                           coconut
D.  com     animal    salary    plant
        a       ant       100
        a       ape
        b       bird      200
        b       .                   banana
        c       cat
        c       .                   coconut
```

35. Given datasets a and b as follows:

```
data a;
input name $ job $;
cards;
ali teacher
carol manager
dave ceo
;
run;
data b ;
input name $ drink $;
cards;
ali milk
carol water
dave juice
;
run;
```

Data set c is created as follows:

```
data c;
set a;
set b;
run;
```

Which of the following is the content of dataset c?

```
A.  name      job           drink
    ali       teacher       milk
    carol     manager       water
    dave      ceo           juice
B.  name      job           drink
    ali       .             milk
    ali       teacher       .
    carol     .             water
    carol     manager       .
    dave      .             juice
    dave      ceo           .
```

C.

name	job	drink
ali	teacher	
ali		milk
carol	manager	
carol		water
dave	ceo	
dave		juice

D.

name	job	drink
ali	teacher	.
ali	.	milk
carol	manager	.
carol	.	water
dave	ceo	.
dave	.	juice

36. Given datasets a and b as follows:

```
data a;
input name $ job $;
cards;
ali teacher
carol manager
dave ceo
;
run;

data b ;
input name $ drink $;
cards;
ali milk
carol water
dave juice
;
run;

data c;
merge a b;
by name;
run;
```

Which of the following is the content of dataset c?

A.

name	job	drink
ali	.	milk
ali	teacher	.
carol	.	water
carol	manager	.
dave	.	juice
dave	ceo	

B.

name	job	drink
ali	teacher	milk

```
    carol     manager       water
    dave      ceo           juice
C.  name      job           drink
    ali       teacher
    ali                     milk
    carol     manager
    carol                   water
    dave      ceo
    dave                    juice

D.  name      job           drink
    ali       teacher       .
    ali       .             milk
    carol     manager       .
    carol     .             water
    dave      ceo           .
    dave      .             juice
```

37. Which one of the following statements is correct when combining datasets using match-merge (merging with a BY statement)?
    A. When the last observation from a BY group in one dataset has been read into the program data vector, SAS retains its values for all variables unique to that dataset until all observations for that BY group have been read from all datasets.
    B. When the last observation from a BY group in one dataset has been read into the program data vector, SAS retains its values for all variables to that dataset until all observations for that BY group have been read from all datasets.
    C. When the first observation from a BY group in one dataset has been read into the program data vector, SAS retains its values for all variables unique to that dataset until all observations for that BY group have been read from all datasets.
    D. When the first observation from a BY group in one dataset has been read into the program data vector, SAS retains its values for all variables to that dataset until all observations for that BY group have been read from all datasets.

38. When updating datasets, using an UPDATE statement, which of the following statement is *not* true?
    A. You work with two datasets.
    B. You can use a BY statement.
    C. The number of observations in the new dataset is the sum of the number of observations in both datasets.
    D. You must not use a BY statement.

39. Given datasets a and b as follows:
```
Data a;
Input name $ salary;
Cards;
Ali 23
Dave 66
;
```

```
run;

data b;
input name $ age sex $;
cards;
bob 55 m
james 44 m
karl 22
;
run;
```

Dataset c is created as follows:
```
Data c;
Update a b;
By name;
Run;
```

Which of the following is the content of dataset c?

A.
name	salary	age	sex
ali	23		
bob	55		m
dave	66		
james	44		m

B.
name	salary	age	sex
ali	23	.	
bob	.	55	m
dave	66	.	
james	.		

C.
name	salary	age	sex
ali	23	.	
bob	.	55	m
dave	66	.	
james	.	44	m

D.
name	salary	age	sex
ali	23		.
bob		55	m
dave	66		.
james		44	m

40. Dataset a has 35 observations, while data set b has 21 observations. How many observations does dataset c have?
```
Data c;
 Set a;
 Set b;
 Run;
```
A. 35
B. 21

C. 56
D. 14

41. Data set a has 23 observations and dataset b has 9 observations. How many observations does dataset 'c' have?
```
Data c;
Merge a b;
Run;
```
A. 32
B. 9
C. 14
D. 23

42. The following DATA step is submitted:
```
Data a;
Input name $ salary;
Cards;
Bob +125000
;
run;
```

Which value is stored in the output dataset?

A.	name	salary
	Bob	125000
B.	name	salary
	Bob	+125000
C.	name	salary
	Bob	(missing value)
D.	name	salary
	missing value)	(missing value)

43. Dataset a has one observation and data set b has two observations. How many observations will be in dataset c which is created in the following DATA step?
```
Data c;
Set a b;
Run;
```
A. 1.
B. 2.
C. 3.
D. No output will be created because of a syntax error.

44. Dataset a and data set b each have a variable called name and are sorted properly. If data set a has 10 observations and data set b has 20 observations, how many observations are in dataset c?
```
data c;
set a b;
by name;
run;
```

A. DATA STEP will not execute because of an error
B. 20.
C. 30.
D. This depends on how many observations match

45. Which one of the following is an INPUT statement option?
    A. Truncover
    B. Missover
    C. Pad
    D. None of the above

46. In your list INPUT statement, if you declare `telephone number` to be numeric, and in the raw data you enclose the `telephone number` value in parantheses, what will be shown in the output dataset for that value?
    A. A period.
    B. Complete value of `telephone number` including parentheses.
    C. SAS will eliminates parentheses and give the complete number as the value of `telephone number`.
    D. No output will be created as the result of a syntax error.

47. If the following DATA step is executed, what will be the message in the log?
    ```
    Data a;
    Input name $ tel;
    Cards;
    David (404)2315566
    ;
    run;
    ```
    A. No message.
    B. *Note*: invalid data for `tel` in line 1. ERROR=1 *N*=1.
    C. *Note*: invalid data for `tel` in line 1.
    D. *Note*: Dataset WORK.A has one observation and two variables.
    E. Both B and D.
    F. None of the above.

48. If the DATA STEP in question 47 is executed, what will be the content of the output dataset?
    A. name   tel
        David   4042315566
    B. name   tel
        David   (404)2315566
    C. name   tel
        David   (missing value)
    D. name   tel
        David   .

49. What will be the output of the following DATA step?
    ```
    Data a;
    Input name $ salary;
    ```

```
Cards;
Roger 100000
Bob
David 200000
;
run;
```

A.
name	salary
Roger	1000000
Bob	.
David	200000

B.
name	salary
Roger	100000
Bob	200000
David	200000

C.
name	salary
Roger	100000
Bob	.

D.
name	salary
Roger	100000
Bob	100000
David	200000

50. Running the DATA step of the previous question, what will be the message in the SAS LOG?
   A. SAS went to a new line when the INPUT statement reached past the end of a line.
   B. SAS brought the value of variable *salary* from line 3 and placed it on line 2.
   C. SAS assumed that the value of variable salary has not changed from line 1.
   D. SAS placed a period for the value of variable salary on line 2 and continued to execute line 3.

51. Given the following line of data:
   Alison 23 George 36.
   Which of the given INPUT statements will produce the given line of data?
   A. input name $ age;
   B. input name $ age @;
   C. input name $ age @@;
   D. input @ name $ age ;

52. With which one of the following INPUT statement can you read nonstandard data?
   A. List
   B. Column
   C. Formatted
   D. All of the above

53. Which of the following is a correct INPUT statement?
   A. Input name $ 12 +4 grade1 comma5 +6 grade2 comma5;
   B. Input name $ 12 +4 grade1 comma5. +6 grade comma5.;
   C. Input name $ 12 +4. grade1 comma5. +6. grade2 comma5.;

 D. Input name $ 12. +4 grade1 comma5. +6 grade2 comma5.;

54. SAS statements are free-formatted. This means that
 A. They can begin and end in any column.
 B. One statement can continue over several lines.
 C. Several statement appear on the same line.
 D. All of the above.

55. When executing a SAS program;
 A. Each step is executed independently.
 B. All steps are executed together.
 C. Only DATA steps are executed independently.
 D. Only PROC steps are executed independently.

56. Which of the following statements names the dataset to be created?
 A. DATA statement
 B. PROC statement
 C. LENGTH statement
 D. None of the above

57. For each field of raw data read into a SAS dataset, you must assign:
 A. A valid SAS variable name
 B. A TYPE
 C. A LENGTH
 D. All of the above

58. Which of the following statements separates "words" in a SAS statement?
 A. A blank
 B. Special characters
 C. Both A and B
 D. Neither A nor B

59. When a SAS program is submitted, which of the following is (are) true?
 A. When a RUN statement is submitted, the entire program executes.
 B. When a DATA statement is submitted, the entire program executes.
 C. When a PROC statement is submitted, the entire program executes.
 D. When a DATA, PROC, or RUN statement is submitted, the entire program executes.

60. Which of the following is (are) correct?
 A. The LIBNAME specifies the file containing the raw data.
 B. The INFILE specifies the file containing the raw data.
 C. Both A and B
 D. Neither A nor B

Practice exam answers

1. C – with LIST input, if a variable is declared to be numeric, but the raw data contain a character in the value (here a dash), then SAS inserts a period for the value of that variable.
2. B – if there is a period for a character variable in the raw data, SAS inserts a blank for the value of that variable in the output dataset.
3. A – if the raw data contains a blank for a character or numeric variable, SAS reads in the next value the in raw data.
4. C – in COLUMN input no placeholder is needed.
5. A – in the COLUMN input, if there is a blank for the value of a numeric variable, then SAS puts a period for the value of that variable.
6. B – in COLUMN input, if there is a blank in the value of a character variable, then the output for the value of that variable is a blank without any error message in the log.
7. D – in FORMATTED input, column pointers are numbers which follow the informat.
8. F – in FORMATTED input, no placeholder is required. Character values can contain blanks, and entire value, or part of a value that can be reread.
9. D – in one DATA STEP, you can use as many INPUT and INFILE statements as you wish.
10. B – INFILE statement can be used only for raw data.
11. E – when using the MISSOVER option in an INFILE statement, the INPUT statement does not jump to the next line and SAS sets the value to "missing".
12. C – PAD adds blanks to the lines of data to fill them to the logical length.
13. A – MISSOVER gives best result with LIST input.
14. B – because PAD adds blanks to fill lines of data, it works correctly and completely with COLUMN input.
15. A – @ holds the input record for execution of the next input statement.
16. C – in the LIST input statement one slash is the default delimiter.
17. B – in the LIST input statement, a missing value must be shown by a period.
18. A – double trailing @ holds the input record for execution of the next input statement.
19. C – both / and # are line pointers.
20. D – #2 indicates that reading of data must begin on the second line of the record and # 4 implies that there are four lines of data per record.
21. C – when using the POINT= option, SAS begins reading the data from the value of the temporary value on the right side of the equal sign to the end of the dataset. It must always be used in a DO loop. It can never be used with a BY or a WHERE statement.
22. C – if you do not use STOP before END, you get an infinite loop.
23. B – if you use a number, on the right side of POINTt=, you get an error message in the log saying "expecting a name".
24. C – this is one-to-one reading. It combines observations from two or more datasets into one observation using two or more SET statements. The number of observations in the output data set is the number of observations in the smallest data set
25. B – this is match – merging. The number of observations in the output dataset is the sum of the largest number of observations in each BY group in all datasets.

26. A – in updating datasets you work with two datasets: one called the "master" dataset and the other, the "transaction" data set. The number of observations in the output data set is the total number of observations in the master dataset and unmatched ones in the transaction dataset.

27. C – this is interleaving. The total number of observations is the sum of the number of observations in both datasets.

28. B – if the length of a variable varies between datasets, SAS takes the length from the first dataset.

29. C – in combining data sets when using SET, MERGE, and UPDATE, many-to-many reading can not be used.

30. D – when combining data sets using SET, MERGE, and UPDATE one-to-many and many-to-one readings cannot be used.

31. A – format, informat, and label of the first dataset overrides the others.

32. B – All observations from the first data set, and then all observations from the second data set and so on.

33. A – sum of observations in both datasets.

34. A.

35. A.

36. B.

37. A.

38. D.

39. C.

40. B – total number of observations is the number of observations from the smallest dataset.

41. D – total number of observations is the number of observations from the largest dataset.

42. A – the plus or minus sign is considered to be part of a number.

43. C – see explanation for question 3.

44. C – when you are using one SET statement (with or without a BY statement) to merge datasets, the number of observations in the output dataset is equal to the total number of observations in both datasets.

45. D – none of these are an INPUT statement option. They are all INFILE statement options.

46. A – see explanation for question 8.

47. E – The message in the log will be: *Note*; Invalid data for `tel` in line 1. `Error = 1` `_N_ = 1`. *Note*: Dataset `WORK.A` has one observation and two variables.

48. D – Since `tel` is a numeric variable and the value in the raw data is character because of parentheses – then SAS puts a period for the value of `tel`.

49. C – Since there is no value for `salary` on line 2 SAS will go to line 3 to read the next value. This value is a character `David`, so SAS inserts a period for the value of `salary` and goes to next the line in order to complete reading the values for line 3. When it hits the semicolon, it terminates the construction of data.

50. A – the message in the log will be "SAS went to a new line when INPUT statement reached past end of a line."

51. C – double trailing @ holds the INPUT record for the execution of the next INPUT statement.

52. C – formatted statement can read nonstandard data.

53. D – `12` and `comma5` are formats, so each must have a period at the end of them.

54. D – SAS statements are free-format; this means that they can begin and end in any column, or that one statement can continue over several lines or that several statements can appear on the line.

55. A – when executing a SAS program, each step is executed separately.
56. A – DATA statement names the dataset you are creating.
57. D – for each field of raw data read into a SAS dataset, you must assign a valid SAS variable name, a type, and a length.
58. C – a blank or special characters separate "words" in SAS statements.
59. D – when a DATA, PROC, or RUN statement is submitted, the previous step executes.
60. B – the INFILE statement specifies the file containing the raw data.

Problems

1. Suppose that a comma is the delimiter in the raw data. Write an INFILE statement to specify this.

2. Suppose you are given a raw data file. Write an INFILE statement to read data from row 3.

3. Suppose that you are given the following raw data and the values are separated by one or more blanks. Variables are job_tit, salary and bonus. Notice that some values are missing and lines are not padded with blanks. Write a DATA STEP to create a SAS dataset.
```
Janitor 17000 859
Gardner 21000
Dentist
Cleaner 19000 1100
```

4. Using the data in problem 3 with job_tit in columns 1—7, salary in columns 9—13 and *bonus* in columns 15—18. Write a data step to read these data correctly.

5. Suppose that you have data from two different sources. Data from source one has a 1 in column 1. Data from source 2 has a 2 in column 1. Write a program to create a dataset using the following data:
```
11 john 1 77
11 88   2 james
22 boby 1 55
22 89   2 opey
```

6. Given the data:
```
john 88 mary 87 bob 99
```
write a program to produce the following ouput:
```
john 88
mary 87
bob 99
```

7. Suppose that you are given a file of data with four records per observation. Write a program to read two variables – say, name and id–from row 1.

8. Repeat problem 7, but use the other line pointer.

9. Given the following two datasets, write a program to combine them so dataset c (below) will be the result:
```
data a;
input part_id $ pt_name $ shelf $;
cards;
a belt front
b washer back
```

```
;
run;

data b;
input part_id $ shelf $;
cards;
a heavey
b light
c medium
;
run;
```
Data set c:

Obs	part_id	pt_name	shelf
1	a	belt	front
2	b	washer	back
3	a		heavy
4	b		light
5	c		medium

10. Given the two datasets in problem 7, write a program to combine them so that data set c (below) will be the result.
    Dataset c:

Obs	part_id	pt_name	shelf
1	a	belt	front
2	a		heavy
3	b	washer	back
4	b		light
5	c		medium

11. Given the two datasets in problem 7, write a program to combine them so that dataset c below will be the result.
    Dataset c:

Obs	part_id	pt_name	shelf
1	a	belt	heavy
2	b	washer	light
3	c		medium

Problem solutions

```
1.  infile 'raw data file' dlm=',';
2.  infile 'raw data file' firstobs=3;
3.  data a;
    infile datalines missover;
    input job_tit $ salary bonus;
    cards;
```

```
janitor 17000 859
gardner 21000
dentist
cleaner 19000 1100
;
run;
```
Output:

	Obs	job_tit	salary	bonus
	1	janitor	17000	859
	2	gardner	21000	.
	3	dentist	.	.
	4	cleaner	19000	1100

4. The solution is the same as that to problem 3 except that instead of INFILE option MISSOVER you need to use the option PAD.

5.
```
data bb;
input @9 source 1. @;
if source=1 then input @1 id 1-2 @4 name $ 4. score 11-12;
else if source=2 then input @1 id 1-2 @4 score 2. @11 name $
5.;
cards;
11 john 1 77
11 88   2 james
22 boby 1 55
22 89   2 opey
;
run;
proc print data=bb;
run;
```

Output:

	Obs	source	id	name	score
	1	1	11	john	77
	2	2	11	jame	88
	3	1	22	boby	55
	4	2	22	opey	89

6.
```
data aa;
input name $ score @@;
cards;
```

```
john 88 mary 87 bob 99
;
run;
```

7.  ```
    data aa;
    input #1 name $ id #4;
    cards;
    john 01
    bob 02
    crol 03
    adam 04
    maggi 05
    nigel 06
    mary 07
    doug 08
    ;
    run;
    ```

8. In the INPUT statement use three slashes (///) instead of #4 and delete #1.

9.  ```
    data c;
    set a b;
    run;
    proc print data=c;
    run;
    ```

10. ```
    data c;
    set a b;
    by part_id;
    run;
    proc print data=c;
    run;
    ```

11. ```
    data c;
    update a b;
    by part_id;
    run;
    proc print data=c;
    run;
    ```

2 Creating Data Structures

Certification objectives

In this chapter you will learn what you need to pass this section of the exam:

- **Creating temporary and permanent SAS datasets**
- **Explaining how the DATA step is compiled and executed**
- **Using DATA step statements to export data to a standard and to a comma-delimited files**
- **Creating and manipulating SAS date values**
- **Understand the role of a BY statement in the DATA step**
- **Controlling which observations and variables in a SAS dataset are processed and output**

In this chapter you will learn about creating temporary and permanent SAS datasets and how to manipulate SAS date, time, and datetime values. You will learn to understand how to control which observations and variables in a SAS dataset are processed and output. In this chapter you will also learn how the DATA step is compiled and executed.

At the end of this chapter you can review the material by reading the two-minute drill, and you can answer the questions to the practice test to evaluate your understanding and retention of the material in this chapter. The answers to these practice test questions are given at the end of the test. Also, a set of problems with solutions are provided for further practice.

2.1 Creating temporary and permanent SAS datasets

This section provides information about names for SAS datasets and describes permanent and temporary dataset names. You give a name to a SAS dataset when you create it. Output SAS datasets, which are created in a DATA step, are named in the DATA statement. If a SAS dataset is created in a PROCEDURE step, it is usually given a name in the PROCEDURE statement or in an output statement. If you forget to specify a name for an output dataset, the SAS system gives it a default name.

When you refer to SAS datasets in your program statements, use a one-level or two-level name depending on the nature of the SAS data library where you store data.

2.1.1 Two-level names

The two-level name is used to create, read, or write to SAS datasets. You create a two-level dataset by giving it a library reference and a name.

In the following example the word *green* is the library reference (`libref`) and *salary* is the name of the permanent SAS dataset. Libref indicates where the new SAS dataset will be stored. When you reference an existing SAS dataset, the libref tells the SAS system where to look for the file.

Example 2.1
```
libname green 'c:\mydata';
Data green.salary;
```

OR
```
proc means data=green.salary;
```

   If you have a raw dataset stored in a file, you can specify that file in an INFILE statement in the DATA step. The INFILE statement must be executed before the INPUT statement.

Example 2.2
```
Data employees;
Infile 'c:\mydata\comempl';
Input name $ salary position $;
Run;
```

   The SAS system reads the data from the *c:\mydata\compempl* file, one data line at a time, and applies the INPUT statement to each record as if it had read it from the instream.

2.1.2 One-level names

When you omit the libref, you create a one-level name for your SAS dataset. This dataset is a temporary one and will be deleted at the end of the SAS job or session. For example

```
data jobs;
```

   Datasets with one-level names are automatically assigned to one of the two special SAS system libraries: WORK and USER.
   One way of creating one-level names is by entering data in a job stream. To do that, you must use a CARDS or a DATALINES statement. These statements must appear at the end of the DATA step. A semicolon must appear on the line following the last data line.

Example 2.3
```
Data salaries;
Input name $ salary;
Datalines;
Jones 42000
Adams 56000
;
run;
```

Instead of DATALINES, you can use CARDS.

2.2 Explaining how the DATA step is compiled and executed

When you submit a DATA step to the SAS system for execution, it is first compiled and then executed.

2.2.1 Compilation phase

When you submit a DATA step, the SAS system checks the syntax of the SAS statements and compiles them; that is, it translates the statements into machine code then creates three items:

(1) Input buffer
(2) Program data vector
(3) Descriptor information.

1. Input buffer. The input buffer is the area of memory into which each record of raw data is read when an INPUT statement executes. Note that an input buffer is created only when raw data are read, not when a SAS dataset is read.

2. *Program data vector*. This is the area of memory where SAS builds your dataset, one observation at a time. When a SAS program executes, the values are read from the input buffer.

3. Descriptor information. This is the information that the SAS system creates and maintains about each SAS dataset, including data set attributes and variables attributes.

2.2.2 Execution phase

By default, a SAS DATA step executes once for each observation being created. The flow of action when the step runs is described below:
1. The DATA statement marks the beginning of a DATA step. Each time the DATA statement executes, a new iteration of the DATA step begins (_N_, the automatic variable whose value is set to the number of times the DATA step has iterated).
2. A data reading statement (INPUT, SET, ...) causes a record of data to be read into the input buffer, or from a SAS dataset into a program data vector.
3. Any subsequent program statements are executed for the current record.
4. At the end of the statements, an output, return, and reset occur automatically. The following actions also take place an observation is written to the SAS dataset; the system returns to the top of the DATA step, then values of variables created by INPUT and ASSIGNMENT statements are reset to missing in the program data vector.
5. SAS system counts another iteration, reads in the next record or observation, and executes the subsequent program statements for the next record.
6. The DATA step terminates when the end-of-file is encountered in a SAS dataset or a raw data file.

The simplest way to execute a DATA (or PROC) step is to put RUN; at the end of the DATA (or PROC) step.
The following sequence of events causes a DATA step to stop executing:

1. If no data reading statement is present (an INPUT, SET, MERGE, UPDATE), it stops after only one iteration.
2. If reading from instream, after last data line.
3. when reading from an external file, after end-of-file is reached.
4. If reading from more than one external file, it stops when end-of-file is reached on any one of the input data files.
5. If a single SET, MERGE, or UPDATE is used, it stops when all the input data sets have been executed.
6. If multiple SET, MERGE, or UPDATE is used, it stops when end-of-file is encountered by any of the data-reading statements.

2.2.3 DATA step boundary and types

The SAS system recognizes several step boundaries for a DATA step:
1. A RUN statement.
2. The semicolon (when CARDS is used) or four semicolons when CARDS4 is used.
3. A DATA statement that begins a new DATA step.
4. A PROC statement.
5. An ENDSAS statement.
6. In noninteractive or batch mode, the end of an input contains a SAS program statement.

TIP: In the following program note that, the OPTIONS statement applies for both DATA steps:

Example 2.4
```
Data s;
Set a;
Options   firstobs=5 obs=44;
Dat t;
Set b;
run;
```

If the OPTIONS statement is placed after the line 'Data t;', it will be effective only for the second data step.

There are four basic types of DATA steps

1.   Data from an external file
2.   Data from instream source
3.   Data existing in SAS datasets
4.   Data generated from programming statements.

2.2.4 When variable values are set to "missing" automatically

The values of all variables (except automatic variables) in the program data vector are initially set to "missing" before the first iteration of the DATA step. Thereafter, variables are set to "missing" depending on the source of the input, either (1) raw data or (2) SAS datasets.

1. Reading raw data. At the beginning of each iteration of DATA step, SAS sets the value of each variable you create in the DATA step to missing with the following exceptions:
a. Variables named in a RETAIN statement
b. Variables created in a SUM statement
c. Data elements in a `_temporary_` array
d. Any variables created with OPTIONS in the FILE or INFILE statement
e. Automatic variables.

2. Reading a SAS dataset. When variables are read with a SET, MERGE, or UPDATE statement, the SAS system sets the values to "missing" only before the first iteration of the DATA step (if a BY statement is present, the variable values are set to "missing" when the BY group changes). Thereafter, the variables retain their values until new values become available.

Variables created with OPTIONS in SET, MERGE, or UPDATE statements also retain their values from one iteration to the next.

TIP: Let's look at the following example and consider a few points.

Example 2.5
```
Data a;
Input name $ income expense;
Loss= income - expense;
Cards;
Ali 12 8
Bob 15 10
Jane 23 5
;
run;
proc print data=a;
run;
```

Output:

```
          The SAS System      11:38 Tuesday, February 8,
          2005

              Obs   name   income   expense Loss
               1    Ali      12        8      4
               2    Bob      15       10      5
               3    Jane     23        5     18
```

1. If in the first line of data the value of the variable *income* is a period (·) instead of 12, the program will work fine. In the output, SAS gives a period for *income* in the first observation and a note in the log saying:

```
NOTE: Missing values were generated as a result of performing
an operation on missing values.
Each place is given by: (Number of times) at (Line):(Column).
1 at 14:14
```

The output for other lines of data is what you expect it to be, as shown below:

```
          The SAS System      11:38 Tuesday, February 8,
          2005

              Obs   name   income   expense Loss
               1    Ali       .        8      .
               2    Bob      15       10      5
               3    Jane     23        5     18
```

2. If you put nothing for 12, that is leave it blank, 8 will be read for income, and the program will go to the next line of data 'Bob' will be considered as the value of expense, and, consequently, an error message will be issued in the log, but the program will work fine for the other observations. This is the output:

```
          The SAS System        11:38 Tuesday, February 8,
          2005
                     Obs   name    income   expense Loss
                     1     Ali     8         .        .
                     2     Jane    23        5        18
```

3. The SAS system accepts signs (— or +) as part of a numeric value but does not accept a slash (/). It gives the correct output for other lines of data except the one(s) with a slash in the value of a numeric variable and gives a note in the log explaining the error,
Note : *invalid data …_Error_ =1.*

4. On the second line of data, if you put a period (·) in place of Bob, the program works fine. In the output, the value of name will be blank in the second observation. The program will calculate Loss for the second observation correctly and for the other observations, values of all variables are also be calculated correctly.

```
Data a;
Input name $ income expense;
Loss= income - expense;
Cards;
Ali 12 8
. 15 10
Jane 23 5
;
run;
proc print data=a;
run;
```

Output:

```
The SAS System      11:38 Tuesday, February 8,
2005
                Obs   name    income    expense  Loss
                1     Ali       12        8        4
                2               15       10        5
                3     Jane      23        5       18
```

2.3 Using the DATA step to export data to standard and comma-delimited raw data file

When creating a report, you can use DATA step to export data to a standard and comma-delimited raw data file without creating a dataset. You must use a PUT statement as explained below:

1. DATA _NULL_ ;. This line begins the DATA step, using the reserved dataset name *NULL*, which indicates that no SAS dataset will be created.
2. Data reading or data-generating. Statements. This line reads data from an external file, from an instream data, or from a SAS data set.
3. FILE statement. This line specifies the file to which the report is to be written
4. PUT statement. This writes lines of the report to the file specified or to the SAS log.

2.3.1 Creating an external file with column-aligned data

With column style output, specify the starting and ending column numbers for the output data after the variable name. The example below uses column style PUT for NAME and AGE.

You can also use control pointers on a PUT statement to align data in columns. In the following program the absolute pointer (@) specifies column 20 as the starting position for SEX. The relative control pointer (+n) helps align WEIGHT and HEIGHT (the data set persons was created before).

Example 2.6
```
data b;
input name $ age sex $ weight height ;
cards;
alice 13 f 84 56.5
barbara 12 f 99 65.4
david 23 m 77 66.5
run;

Data _nul _l;
Set b;
File log;
Put name 1-8 age 13-15 @20 sex +5 weight 5.1 height;
Run;

Log:
alice         13     f        84.056.5
```

```
barbara     12     f     99.065.4
david       23     m     77.066.5
```

Example 2.7
In the following example a delimited file is created using a PUT statement, generating a file whose values are separated by the specified delimiter.

```
data address;
input name $ zipcode number;
cards;
lara 30357 82
boby 30309 23
;
run;

Data _null_;
Set address;
File log dlm='/';
Put name zipcode number ;
Run;
```

Log:
```
lara/30357/82
boby/30309/23
```

2.4 Creating and manipulating SAS date values

SAS processes calendar date values by converting dates to integers representing the number of days between January 1, 1960 and a specified date. For example, the following values represent July 26, 1989:
```
072689 , 26jul89 , 892607 , 7/26/89 , 26jul1989 , 26 jul 1989.
```

The SAS date value representing July 26, 1989 is 10799. In other examples, for January 1, 1959, the SAS date value is –365. For January 1, 1960, the SAS date value is 0; and for July 4, 1776, the SAS date value is –67019

Example 2.8
```
data days;
input date mmddyy8.;
cards;
07/26/89
;
run;
proc print data=days;
run;
```

Output:

```
         The SAS System        11:38 Tuesday, February 8,
         2005
                      Obs      date
                      1       10799
```

Using another format for variable *date, we obtain*

```
data days;
input date date8.;
cards;
26jul89
;
run;
proc print data=days;
run;
```

This produces same output as before:

```
         The SAS System        11:38 Tuesday, February 8,
         2005
                      Obs      date
                      1       10799
```

SAS accepts two-digit or four-digit year values. The default value is 1900.

2.4.1 Processing time data
SAS processes time data similar to dates, converting a specific time to an integer representing the number of seconds since midnight of the current day. For example, the time value for 9:30 am is 34200.

Example 2.9
```
data time;
input time time5.;
cards;
9:30
;
run;
proc print data=time;
run;
```

Output:

```
                The SAS System        11:38 Tuesday, February 8,
                2005
                            Obs      time
                            1       34200
```

2.4.2 Processing datetime values

SAS datetime values are integers representing the number of seconds between midnight January 1, 1960 and a specified date. For example, the datetime value for 11:3am on 8feb2005 is 1423481880.

Example 2.10

```
data datetime;
input datetime datetime22.;
cards;
08feb05 11:38
;
run;
proc print data=datetime;
run;
```

Output:

```
                The SAS System        11:38 Tuesday, February 8,
                2005
                            Obs      datetime
                            1       1423481880
```

Example 2.11

```
Data m;
Input region $ monthly mmddyy8.;
new_m=monthly - 45;
Cards;
North 11-24-90
South 12-28-90
East 12-03-90
;

proc print data=m;
format monthly new_m date8.;
run;
```

Output:

```
                The SAS System        11:38 Tuesday, February 8,
                2005
                            Obs    region    monthly    new_m
                            1      North     24NOV90    10OCT90
                            2      South     28DEC90    13NOV90
                            3      East      03DEC90    19OCT90
```

2.5 Understanding the role of a BY statement in the DATA step

The BY statement is used in DATA steps, and PROC steps.

Before you process one or more SAS datasets using grouped or ordered data, you must sort them in a predictable and corresponding pattern (e.g, ascending, descending). The SAS system detects the pattern by tracking the values of one or more temporary variables called "FIRST.variable" and "LAST.variable". You can use the SORT procedure to change the physical order of the observations in the dataset. You can put the observations in the order you want by (1) using a BY statement or (2) creating an index for the dataset.

Example 2.12
```
Proc sort data=a out=b;
By name;
Run;
```

If you omit the BY statement, you will get an error saying: *"no BY variable used"* with no output. The output of the program is the data set b.
Note that PROC SORT does not print the output automatically.
To print the dataset b, you must use PROC PRINT:

```
Proc print data=b;
Run;
```

2.5.1 Understanding the BY group

There are three concepts to understand:
1. BY variable—is a variable named in a BY statement
2. BY value—the value or formatted value of a BY variable
3. BY group—all observations with the same BY value

2.5.2 How the DATA step identifies the BY group

SAS identifies the beginning and the end of each BY group by creating two temporary variables for each BY variable: FIRST.variable and LAST.variable. These variables are not added to the output.

When an observation is the first observation in a BY group, the value of FIRST.variable is set to 1. For all other observations in the BY group, the value of FIRST.variable is 0. Likewise, if an observation is the last in a BY group, the value of LAST.variable is set to 1. For all other observations in the BY group, LAST.variable is 0.

Example 2.13
By state city zip;

State	city	zip	street	FIRST.state	LAST.state	FIRST.ciy	LAST.city	FIRST.zip	LAST.zip
AL	Tucs	85	Glen	1	1	1	1	1	1
GA	Nam	33	Tom	1	0	1	0	1	0
GA	Nam	33	Sey	0	0	0	0	0	0
GA	Nam	33	Ric	0	0	0	0	0	1
GA	Nam	34	Yon	0	0	0	0	1	0
GA	Nam	34	Dum	0	1	0	1	0	1

2.6 Controling which variables and observations in a SAS data set are processed

If you have two or more datasets and you would like to control which observation from any one of the datasets is entered into the new dataset, you can use IN= variables.

The IN= dataset option is used in the SET, MERGE, or UPDATE statement to create and name a variable that indicates whether the dataset contributed.

Example 2.14
Let's look at the following example where we merge two datasets, assuming that we have two SAS datasets, a and b:

```
data a;
input id gender $ state $;
cards;
1 M NY
2 F NJ
3 F NJ
4 M NY
5 M NY
;

data b;
input id depart $ salary;
datalines;
1 parts 21
2 sales 45
3 parts 20
5 sales 35
;
run;
data ab;
merge a b(in=emp);
by id;
if emp=1;
run;
```

```
proc print data=ab;
run;
```

Output:

```
          The SAS System      11:38 Tuesday, February 8,
          2005

               Obs  id  gender  state  depart  salary
                1    1     M      NY    parts     21
                2    2     F      NJ    sales     45
                3    3     F      NJ    parts     20
                4    5     M      NY    sales     35
```

In the program above, the variable name following the `in=` data set option, emp in this case, refers to a logical variable that will be created with a value of true (1) or false (0). As each observation is built, if data set b has data to contribute, emp will equal 1; if not, emp will equal 0. These `in=` variables are temporary in that they exist only during the execution of DATA step.

The resulting dataset ab contains observations for ids 1,2,3,5.

If you would like to select observations which are in both datasets a and b proceed as follows:

Example 2.15

```
Data both;
Merge a(in=dem) b(in=emp);
By id;
If dem=1 and emp=1;
Run;
```

Output:

```
          The SAS System      11:38 Tuesday, February 8,
          2005

               Obs  id  gender  state  depart  salary
                1    1     M      NY    parts     21
                2    2     F      NJ    sales     45
                3    3     F      NJ    parts     20
                4    5     M      NY    sales     35
```

TIP: In the program above , if you use the following line, it should work fine:

```
If dem and emp;
```
. If you have a third dataset called c then use this line:

```
Merge a(in=dem) b(in=emp) c(in=ham);
```

If you use a WHERE statement instead of an IF statement , you get an error with no output.

2.6.1 Differences between IF and WHERE statements

Although it seems that IF and WHERE statements are the same, they are not. Their main differences are:

1. IF can't be used in PROC step.
2. IF is executable, while WHERE is not.
3. WHERE can be used in both DATA step and PROC step.
4. WHERE statement is more efficient than IF statement (WHERE checks validity of the conditions before bringing observations into the program data vector, while IF does it after observations are read into the program data vector).
    The following operators are used only with the WHERE expression: BETWEEN-AND, LIKE, SOUND LIKE, CONTAIN, IS NULL, or IS MISSING.

`Where empnum occurs between 500 and 600;` Indicates that the employee number is between 500 and 600
`Where lastname like N%;` which indicates that surname begins with `N`.
`Where company contain bay;` which indicates that the name of the company contains the three letter word `bay`
`Where idnum is missing;` which indicates that the idnum is missing.
`Where name is null;` which indicates that the name does not exist.

2.6.2 Incorrect use of IF statement

Look at the following two lines of code:

```
If score lt 65 then grade=0;       WRONG WAY
If 0 le score lt 65 then grade=0;    CORRECT WAY
```

The first statement above assigns a value of zero to the variable grade for any observation that is missing a value for score. This is the way in which SAS stores missing values. The SAS system assumes missing values are smaller than any negative number, and therefore, if the value for score is missing, the grade receives a value of zero.

2.6.3 WHEN an alternative to IF-THEN/ELSE coding

Another way of writing a conditional statement is by using the WHEN statement.
The following example makes it clear how to use WHEN.

Example 2.16
```
Data h;
Set grades;
Select;
When(0 le score lt 69) grade=0;
When(69 le score lt 79) grade=1;
..

..
```

```
when(score ge 90) grade=4;
end;
run;
```

*TIP: If a **numeric** variable you use contains a period(.) or a character, the program will work fine but in the place of that variable in the observation, SAS will place a period(.) in the output. Consider the following program:*

Example 2.17
```
data k;
input name $ state $ zip;
cards;
john ga 30303
mary nc .
fred ca 30-3
;
run;
proc print data=k;
run;
```

Output:

```
        The SAS System        11:38 Tuesday, February 8, 2005
                    Obs     name     state      zip
                    1       john     ga         30303
                    2       mary     nc            .
                    3       fred     ca            .
```

If the value of a character variable is a period, the program will work fine, but in the output, you get a blank on that observation. In the program above suppose that instead of John, we use a period. Then the output will look like this:

```
      The SAS System      11:38 Tuesday, February 8, 2005
                    Obs    name    state     zip
                    1               ga       30303
                    2      mary     nc         .
                    3      fred     ca         .
```

Chapter summary

This chapter explained how to create temporary and permanent SAS datasets and how to manipulate and work with SAS date, time, and datetime values. Chapter 2 also described different ways to control which observations and variables in a SAS dataset are processed and output. The chapter also explained how the DATA step is compiled and executed.

Two-minute drill

- There are two kinds SAS datasets: temporary and permanent.
- To create a permanent (two-level) SAS dataset, you must use libref.
- When creating a SAS dataset, if you do not use a libref, you are creating a one level (temporary) dataset.
- Temporary SAS datasets are deleted at the end of a SAS job or session.
- Temporary SAS datasets are assigned to SAS system libraries WORK or USER.
- When using a CARDS or DATALINES statement, a semicolon must appear on the line following the last line of data.
- A data reading statement causes a record of data to be read into the input buffer, or from a SAS dataset into a program data vector.
- When the compilation phase of a program is completed, the SAS system creates three items: (1) input buffer, (2) program data vector (PDV), and (3) descriptor information.
- By default, a SAS datastep executes once for each observation created.
- The DATA statement marks the beginning of a DATA step.
- At the end of the statement an output, return, and reset occur automatically.
- Values of variables created by INPUT and ASSIGNMENT statements are reset to "missing" in the program data vector.
- The DATA step terminates when end-of-file is encountered in a SAS dataset or a raw data file.
- SAS system recognizes several step boundaries for a DATA step: (1) a RUN statement, (2) the semicolon (when CARDS is used) or four semicolons when CARDS4 is used, (3) a DATA statement that begins a new data step, (4) a PROC statement, (5) an ENDSAS statement, (6) in an interactive mode, the end of an input file containing SAS programming statement.
- There are four types of data statements: (1) data from an external file, (2) instream data, (3) data from existing datasets, (4) data generated from programming statements.
- What causes a DATA step to stop executing: (1) if no data-reading statement is present; (2) if reading from instream, after last data line; (3) if reading from external file, after end-of-file is reached; (4) if reading from more than one external file, when end-of-file is reached on any of the input data files; (5) if single SET, MERGE, or UPDATE is used, when all the input data sets have been executed; (6) if multiple SET, MERGE, or UPDATE is used, when end-of-file is encountered by any data-reading statement.
- The SAS system accepts a period or a dash (-) as part of a numeric variable.
- The values of all variables (except automatic variables) in the program data vector are initially set to missing before the first iteration of DATA step.
- When variables are read with a SET, MERGE, or UPDATE statement, after the first iteration, variables retain their values until new values become available.
- The SAS system processes calendar date values by converting dates to integers representing number of days between January 1, 1960 and a specified date.
- The SAS system processes time data values by converting a specified time to an integer representing the number of seconds since midnight of the current day.
- The SAS system's datetime values are integers representing the number of seconds between midnight January 1, 1960 and a specified datetime.
- You can use the SORT procedure to change the physical order of observations in a dataset.

- BY group is used in (1) DATA stepand (2) PROC step.
- Before you process one or more SAS datasets using grouped or ordered data, you must sort them in a predictable pattern (e.g., ascending or descending).
- The SAS system identifies the beginning and The end of each BY group by creating two temporary variables for each variable: FIRST.variable and LAST.variable.
- FIRST.variable and LAST.variable are not added to output.
- The SAS system considers missing values smaller than any negative number.
- The WHERE statement is more efficient than IF statement.
- The IF statement cannot be used in a PROC step.
- IF is executable; WHERE is not.
- WHERE can be used in both DATA step and PROC step.

Assessment exam

1. Which one should be executed first, INPUT or INFILE statement?
2. In a name of a permanent SAS dataset, what does libref indicate?
3. If you have a raw dataset, where should you specify it?
4. Where is a one-level SAS dataset automatically assigned?
5. When you use a job stream to enter data, what marks the end of DATALINES?
6. At the end of the compilation phase, what is (are) created by the SAS system?
7. When is an input buffer created?
8. In which part of memory does SAS build the dataset?
9. What marks the beginning of a DATA step?
10. By default, how many times does a DATA step execute for each observation being created?
11. What is the simplest way to cause a DATA step to execute?
12. Name two data-reading statements.
13. If a single SET, MERGE, or UPDATE is used, when does the DATA step stop executing?
14. How does SAS recognize a DATA step boundary? Name two of them.
15. How many types of DATA steps are there?
16. In a DATA step, which SAS reserved name would you use if you don't want to create a SAS data set?
17. SAS processes calendar date values by converting dates to integers representing number of days from what date?
18. SAS converts time to an integer representing number of seconds from what time?
19. How would you change the physical order of the observations in a dataset?
20. How does SAS identify the beginning and the end of each BY group?
21. Suppose that you are using a SET, MERGE, or UPDATE statement to create a new dataset. How would you control which observation is being contributed from which of the datasets?
22. Can you use an IF statement in a PROC step?
23. Which one of IF or WHERE statement is more efficient?
24. Can you use a WHERE statement in a DATA step?
25. What is an alternative to an IF-THEN/ELSE statement?

Assessment exam answers

1. INFILE statement.
2. It indicates where the SAS dataset will be stored.
3. In INFILE statement.
4. It is assigned to one of the two libraries WORK or USER.
5. A semicolon after last line of data.
6. Three items are created: input buffer, program data vector, and descriptor information.
7. It is created only when raw data are read.
8. In program data vector.
9. A DATA statement.
10. Once.
11. To put a RUN; at the end of DATA step.
12. INPUT and SET.

13. When all the input datasets have been executed.
14. A RUN statement, a DATA statement that begins a new DATA step.
15. There are four of them.
16. The reserved name *NULL*.
17. From January 1, 1960.
18. From midnight of the current day.
19. Use SORT procedure.
20. By creating two temporary variables: FIRST.variable and LAST.variable.
21. You must use the IN= dataset option.
22. No.
23. WHERE statement is more efficient.
24. Yes.
25. WHEN statement.

Practice exam

1. Which of the following is correct:
   A. In a program, an INFILE statement comes after an INPUT statement.
   B. In a program, an INFILE statement comes before an INPUT statement.
   C. In a program, an INFILE statement comes on the same line as an INPUT statement.
   D. An INFILE statement is only for compilation phase.

2. The complete name of every SAS dataset has how many parts?
   A. One part
   B. Two parts
   C. Three parts
   D. Four parts

3. Which of the following is (are) element(s) of a complete name of every SAS dataset?
   A. libref
   B. data-set-name
   C. member type
   D. All of the above
   E. A and B only

4. When the compilation phase is finished without any error, SAS creates
   A. An input buffer
   B. A program data vector
   C. Descriptor information
   D. All of the above
   E. A—C apply for execution phase, not compilation.

5. When the program executes, the data values are read from the
   A. Data vector
   B. Descriptor information
   C. Input buffer
   D. Any of the above

6. Which of the following marks the beginning of a DATA step?
   A. INPUT statement
   B. INFILE statement
   C. DATA statement
   D. PROC statement

7. At the end of the DATA, statement, which of the following occurs automatically?
   A. An output
   B. Return
   C. Reset
   D. All of the above
   E. Only A and B

8. Which of the following terminates the datastep?
   A. When end-of-file is encountered

B.   When an END statement is encountered
C.   Any of the above

9.   Which of the following is recognized by SAS as a boundary for a DATA step?
A.   An END statement
B.   A RUN statement
C.   A FINISH statement
D.   All of the above
E.   None of the above
F.   A and B only

10. Which of the following is recognized by SAS as a boundary for a DATA step?
A.   A PROC statement
B.   A DATA statement that begins a new DATA step
C.   Both A and B
D.   None of the above

11. In the following, `options` is for which of the DATA steps?
```
Data newempl;
Set employs;
Options firstobs=5 obs=99;
Data newjobs;
Set jobs;
Run;
```
A.   For both DATA steps
B.   Only for the first one
C.   Only for the second one
D.   Neither of them; it is not in a proper place.

12. What causes a DATA step to stop executing?
A.   If reading from instream data after the last data line
B.   If no data reading statement is present
C.   If reading from more than one external file, when end-of-file is reached on any one of the input data files
D.   All of the above

13. In question 11, if the `options` statement appears after the line `data newjobs;` then 'options' would be for:
A.   The first DATA step only
B.   The second DATA step only
C.   Both DATA steps
D.   Neither, it will create an error message in the log

14. The SAS system data value representing January 1, 1959 is
A.   0
B.   365
C.   −365
D.   010159

15. The SAS system data value representing July 4, 1776 is
    A. 0
    B. 67019
    C. –67019
    D. –1776

16. The SAS system converts a specific time to an integer representing number of seconds since
    A. Midnight of previous day
    B. Midday of previous day
    C. Midnight of current day
    D. Midday of current day

17. The SAS system converts datetime values to an integer representing the number of seconds since
    A. January 1, 1959
    B. January 1, 1960
    C. January 1, 1969
    D. January 1, 1970

18. Which one of the following line of code is correct?
    A. `if score lt 59 then grade=0;`
    B. `if 0 lt score lt 59 then grade=0;`
    C. Both A and B
    D. Neither A nor B

19. The SAS system stores missing values to be:
    A. Smaller than any negative value
    B. Zero
    C. Less than –99
    D. Less than or equal to –999

20. In the following program
    ```
    Data emploee;
    Merge newemp oldemp(in=emp);
    By id;
    Run;
    ```
    Which of the following is correct about the variable *emp*?
    A. It is a temporary variable.
    B. It exists only during execution time of DATA step.
    C. It exists only exist during compilation time of DATA step.
    D. It is a permanent variable in the `newemp` dataset
    E. It is a permanent variable in the `oldemp` dataset
    F. A and B.
    G. B and C.

21. Which one of the statements is correct with regard to IF and WHERE statements?

A. IF is executable; WHERE is not
B. WHERE can be used in both DATA step and PROC step
C. IF cannot be used in PROC step
D. All of the above
E. Only A and B
F. Only B and C

Practice exam answers

1. A
2. A
3. D
4. D
5. A
6. C
7. D
8. A
9. B
10. C
11. A
12. D
13. B
14. C
15. C
16. C
17. B
18. B
19. A
20. F
21. D

Problems

1. You have a dataset called `printed` that has variables `title`, `publisher`, `price`. Generate a file whose values are separated by an asterisk (*).

2. Suppose that today is February 10, 2005 and you were born on September 10 1980. Write a program to calculate your age.

3. You are given the following dataset, which contains variables `name` and `salary`. Arrange data in ascending order of salary.
   ```
   Jones  38000
   Green  34500
   King   87900
   White  29000
   ```

4. You are given the following dataset, which has variables `name, salary, date_hire`. Write a program to keep the first appearance of each name.
   ```
   Jones  38000  10/10/99
   Jones  44900  12/03/09
   Green  34500  12/06/98
   Green  49000  11/11/03
   Green  51000  12/12/04
   King   87900  03/03/99
   White  29000  09/09/99
   ```

5. You are given the dataset of problem 4 and the dataset below. Merge the two by name only when the second dataset is contributing. The second dataset has `name` and `date_birth` as its variables.
   ```
   Jones  01/01/80
   White  10/10/70
   ```

6. You are given the data set below; the variables in the dataset are `name` and `grade`. Write a program to change grades between 90 to 100 to A and delete the rest.
   ```
   bnarnes  98
   brown    87
   davis    90
   moore    45
   ```

7. Write a SAS program to calculate the number of seconds between 7:20 am and 7:25 am.

8. Write a SAS program to calculate the number of seconds between the following two date-time values: 12/02/05, 7:25 am and 11/02/05, 7:20 am.

Problem solutions

1. ```
   data _null_;
   libname a 'c:\mydata';
   set printed;
   file log dlm='*';
   put title publisher price;
   run;
   ```

2. ```
   data age;
   input today mmddyy8.;
   age=(today - '10sep1980'd)/365;
   cards;
   02/10/05
   ;
   run;
   proc print data=age;
   run;
   ```

   Output:

   ```
   The SAS System      07:09 Thursday, February 10,
   2005
                                Obs    today      age
   ```

3. ```
   data a;
   input name $ salary;
   datalines;
   Jones 38000
   Green 34500
   King 87900
   White 29000
   ;
   run;
   proc sort data=a out=b;
   by salary;
   run;
   proc print data=b;
   run;
   ```
   ```

4.
```
data cc;
input name $ salary date_hire mmddyy8.;
cards;
Jones 38000 10/10/99
Jones 44900 12/03/09
Green 34500 12/06/98
Green 49000 11/11/03
Green 51000 12/12/04
King 87900 03/03/99
White 29000 09/09/99
;
run;
proc sort data=cc out=dd;
by name ;
run;
data ee;
set dd;
by name;
if first.name;
run;
proc print data=ee;
run;
```

Output:

```
The SAS System     07:09 Thursday, February 10, 2005

date_

           Obs    name     salary     hire
           1      Green     34500    14219
           2      Jones     38000    14527
           3      King      87900    14306
           4      White     29000    14496
```

5.
```
data cc;
input name $ salary date_hire mmddyy8.;
cards;
Jones 38000 10/10/99
Jones 44900 12/03/09
Green 34500 12/06/98
Green 49000 11/11/03
Green 51000 12/12/04
King 87900 03/03/99
White 29000 09/09/99
;
run;
```

```
data name ;
input name $ date_birth ddmmyy8.;
cards;
Jones 01/01/80
White 10/10/70
;
run;

data merged;
merge cc name(in=mm);
if mm;
run;
proc print data=merged;
run;
```

Output:

```
The SAS System      07:09 Thursday, February 10, 2005
                                              date_
date_
                  Obs   name    salary   hire   birth
                  1     Jones   38000    14527  7305
                  2     White   44900    18234  3935
```

6.  ```
    data score;
    input name $ grade;
    datalines;
    bnarnes 98
    brown 87
    davis 90
    moore 45
    ;
    run;

    data new_grade;
    set score;
    if 90 le grade le 100 then grade=4;
    else if grade le 90 then delete;
    run;
    proc print data=new_grade;
    run;
    ```
    ```

Output:

```
The SAS System        07:09 Thursday, February 10,
2005

                          Obs      name
                        grade
```

7.  ```
    data a;
    input time1 time5. time2 time5.;
    seconds=time1 - time2;
    cards;
    7:20 7:25
    ;
    run;
    proc print data=a;
    run;
    ```

    Output:

    ```
    The SAS System    08:26 Friday, February 11, 2005
                            Obs      time1      time2
                          seconds
    ```

8.  ```
    data b;
    input datetime1 datetime13. datetime2 datetime13.;
    seconds=datetime1 - datetime2;
    cards;
    12feb05 7:25 11feb05 7:20
    ;
    run;
    proc print data=b;
    run;
    ```

    Output:

    ```
    The SAS System     08:26 Friday, February 11, 2005
                Obs   datetime1   datetime2 seconds
                 1    1423812300  1423725600  86700
    ```

3   Managing Data

Certification objectives

In this chapter you will learn what you need to pass this section of the exam:

- **Investigating SAS data libraries using Base SAS utility procedures**
- **Using SAS procedures to investigate and evaluate the quality of data**
- **Sorting observations in a SAS dataset**
- **Modifying variable attributes using options and statements in the DATA step**
- **Conditionally executing SAS statements**
- **Using assignment statements in the DATA step**
- **Accumulating subtotals and totals using DATA step statements**
- **Using SAS functions to manipulate character data, numeric data, and SAS date values**
- **Using SAS functions to convert character data to numeric and vice versa**
- **Processing data using DO loops**
- **Processing data using SAS ARRAYS**

In this chapter you will learn how to use different SAS procedures in order to investigate and evaluate quality of data. You will learn how to modify variables attributes using options and statements in the DATA step. You will also learn how to use DO loops and SAS ARRAYS to process data.

At the end of this chapter you can review its material by reading the two-minute drill and taking the practice test to see how well you understand the material. The answer to these questions are provided at the end of the test. A set of problems with solutions are also provided for further practice.

3.1 Investigating SAS data libraries using Base SAS utility procedures

A utility procedure performs a specific type of intermediate processing or data manipulation. According to SAS Institute literature there are 14 utility procedures. We will look at the following 5, which are most commonly used and are essential for passing the SAS exam:
1. DATASETA—manages a SAS data library
2. CONTENTS—describes the contents of a SAS library or a specified member of the library
3. SORTS—sorts a SAS data set according to one or more variables
4. COPY—copies a SAS data library or selected members of the library
5. FORMAT—defines output formats for labeling values and informats for reading data

3.1.1 PROC DATASETS

Use PROC DATASETS to *list*, *copy*, *remov*, or *delete* SAS files. Using this procedure, you can manage indices, append SAS data sets in a SAS data library, and change variable information such as *name*, *format*, *informat* and *label*. This procedure also provides all capabilities of the APPEND, CONTENTS and COPY procedures. The SAS system recognizes the primary PROC DATASETS statement as an implied RUN statement.

Example 3.1
```
libname a 'c:\mydata';
proc datasets lib=a;
```
Notice that we do not need a RUN statement to execute this procedure. The SAS log gives the name of all SAS datasets in the library called mydata:

Log:

```
1    libname a'c:\mydata';
NOTE: Libref A was successfully assigned as follows:
      Engine:        V8
      Physical Name: c:\mydata
2    proc datasets lib=a;
                                    -----Directory-----
                            Libref:        A
                            Engine:        V8
                            Physical Name: c:\mydata
                            File Name:     c:\mydata
                                                 File
                   #  Name                Memtype  Size  Last Modified

                   1  AE2                 DATA     5120  18OCT2001:16:49:46
                   2  BOOKS               DATA     9216  05OCT2003:09:16:22
                   3  CIRCUL              DATA     9216  24FEB2002:11:28:58
                   4  CONTINENTS          DATA    13312  21AUG2002:19:11:38
                   5  COUNTRIES           DATA    37888  21AUG2002:19:11:38
                   6  DISTRIB             DATA    13312  24FEB2002:11:28:58
                   7  EMPLOYEES           DATA    13312  24FEB2002:10:28:12
                   8  FEATURES            DATA    25600  21AUG2002:19:11:38
                   9  ITEMS               DATA    17408  24FEB2002:10:28:12
                  10  LAB2                DATA     5120  18OCT2001:16:43:24
                  11  OILPROD             DATA     5120  21AUG2002:19:11:38
                  12  OILRSRVS            DATA     5120  21AUG2002:19:11:38
                  13  ORDERS              DATA     5120  24FEB2002:11:28:58
                  14  POSTALCODES         DATA     5120  21AUG2002:19:11:38
                  15  UNITEDSTATES        DATA    13312  21AUG2002:19:11:38
                  16  USCITYCOORDS        DATA     9216  21AUG2002:19:11:38
                  17  WORLDCITYCOORDS     DATA    17408  21AUG2002:19:11:38
                  18  WORLDTEMPS          DATA     9216  21AUG2002:19:11:38
```

Now let's use this procedure and change the name of the first dataset AE2 to AE3 in the above library, displayed.

Example 3.2
```
libname a 'c:\mydata';
proc datasets lib=a;
change ae2=ae3;
```

Notice that the name of data set AE2 is changed to AE3.

Log:

```
proc datasets lib=a;
```

```
                              -----Directory-----
                              Libref:           A
                              Engine:           V8
                              Physical Name:  c:\mydata
                              File Name:      c:\mydata
                                               File
              #   Name           Memtype       Size   Last Modified

              1   AE3            DATA          5120   18OCT2001:16:49:46
              2   BOOKS          DATA          9216   05OCT2003:09:16:22
              3   CIRCUL         DATA          9216   24FEB2002:11:28:58
              4   CONTINENTS     DATA         13312   21AUG2002:19:11:38
              5   COUNTRIES      DATA         37888   21AUG2002:19:11:38
              6   DISTRIB        DATA         13312   24FEB2002:11:28:58
              7   EMPLOYEES      DATA         13312   24FEB2002:10:28:12
              8   FEATURES       DATA         25600   21AUG2002:19:11:38
              9   ITEMS          DATA         17408   24FEB2002:10:28:12
             10   LAB2           DATA          5120   18OCT2001:16:43:24
             11   OILPROD        DATA          5120   21AUG2002:19:11:38
             12   OILRSRVS       DATA          5120   21AUG2002:19:11:38
             13   ORDERS         DATA          5120   24FEB2002:11:28:58
             14   POSTALCODES    DATA          5120   21AUG2002:19:11:38
             15   UNITEDSTATES   DATA         13312   21AUG2002:19:11:38
             16   USCITYCOORDS   DATA          9216   21AUG2002:19:11:38
             17   WORLDCITYCOORDS DATA        17408   21AUG2002:19:11:38
             18   WORLDTEMPS     DATA          9216   21AUG2002:19:11:38
10    changee ae2=ae3;
```

Let's delete dataset AE3:

Example 3.3
```
libname b 'c:\mydata';
proc datasets lib=b;
delete ae3;
```

Following are the contents of the SAS log. Notice that the dataset AE3 has been deleted.

Log:

```
31   proc datasets lib=b;
                                       -----Directory-----
                               Libref:        B
                               Engine:        V8
                               Physical Name: c:\mydata
                               File Name:     c:\mydata
                                              File
                     #   Name               Memtype    Size   Last Modified

                     1   BOOKS              DATA       9216   05OCT2003:09:16:22
                     2   CIRCUL             DATA       9216   24FEB2002:11:28:58
                     3   CONTINENTS         DATA      13312   21AUG2002:19:11:38
                     4   COUNTRIES          DATA      37888   21AUG2002:19:11:38
                     5   DISTRIB            DATA      13312   24FEB2002:11:28:58
                     6   EMPLOYEES          DATA      13312   24FEB2002:10:28:12
                     7   FEATURES           DATA      25600   21AUG2002:19:11:38
                     8   ITEMS              DATA      17408   24FEB2002:10:28:12
                     9   LAB2               DATA       5120   18OCT2001:16:43:24
                    10   OILPROD            DATA       5120   21AUG2002:19:11:38
                    11   OILRSRVS           DATA       5120   21AUG2002:19:11:38
                    12   ORDERS             DATA       5120   24FEB2002:11:28:58
                    13   POSTALCODES        DATA       5120   21AUG2002:19:11:38
                    14   UNITEDSTATES       DATA      13312   21AUG2002:19:11:38
                    15   USCITYCOORDS       DATA       9216   21AUG2002:19:11:38
                    16   WORLDCITYCOORDS    DATA      17408   21AUG2002:19:11:38
                    17   WORLDTEMPS         DATA       9216   21AUG2002:19:11:38
```

Use the DATASETS procedure to manage a SAS data library. When using PROC DATASETS, groups of statements can execute without a RUN statement.
The following example shows how to copy the datasets from one library to another.

Example 3.4
```
libname old 'c:\mydata';
libname new 'c:\tempdata';
proc datasets lib=old;
copy out=new ;
run;
```

Notice that this program copies SAS datasets from library *old* to library *new*. It does not copy SAS programs or text data.
To move a temporary dataset to a permanent library, see the example below.

Example 3.5
```
data de;
input name $ sal;
cards;
aa 45
bb 67
;
run;
```

```
libname old 'c:\mydata';
proc datasets lib=work;
copy out=old;
run;
```

This is part of SAS log:

```
48   libname old 'c:\mydata';
NOTE: Libname OLD refers to the same physical library as A.
NOTE: Libref OLD was successfully assigned as follows:
     Engine:        V8
     Physical Name: c:\mydata
49   *libname new 'c:\work';
50   proc datasets lib=work;
                                       -----Directory-----
                   Libref:      WORK
                   Engine:      V8
                   Physical Name: C:\windows\TEMP\SAS Temporary Files\_TD43337
                   File Name:   C:\windows\TEMP\SAS Temporary Files\_TD43337
                                              File
                   #  Name   Memtype   Size  Last Modified

                   1  DE     DATA      5120  14FEB2005:15:51:56
51   copy out=old;
52   run;
NOTE: Copying WORK.DE to OLD.DE (memtype=DATA).
NOTE: There were 2 observations read from the data set WORK.DE.
NOTE: The data set OLD.DE has 2 observations and 2 variables.
```

3.1.2 PROC CONTENTS

This procedure provides information for SAS datasets or libraries , and can be useful for documentation purposes. The following example shows the basic syntax for PROC contents.

Example 3.6
```
libname a 'c:\mydata';
proc contents data=a.books;
run;
```

Output:

```
The SAS System       14:46 Wednesday, December 10, 2003
                             The CONTENTS Procedure
          Data Set Name: A.BOOKS                       Observations:      9
          Member Type:   DATA                          Variables:         7
          Engine:        V8                             Indexes:           0
          Created:       9:16 Sunday, October 5, 2003  Observation Length:
56
          Last Modified: 9:16 Sunday, October 5, 2003  Deleted
Observations: 0
          Protection:                                  Compressed:       NO
          Data Set Type:                               Sorted:           YES
          Label:
                        -----Engine/Host Dependent Information-----
                  Data Set Page Size:           8192
                  Number of Data Set Pages:     1
                  First Data Page:              1
                  Max Obs per Page:             145
                  Obs in First Data Page:       9
                  Number of Data Set Repairs:   0
                  File Name:                    c:\mydata\books.sas7bdat
                  Release Created:              8.0202M0
                  Host Created:                 WIN_98
                  -----Alphabetic List of Variables and Attributes-----
               #  Variable     Type    Len    Pos    Format
Informat

               4  author       Char     8      24
               1  cost         Num      8       0    DOLLAR9.2
DOLLAR9.2
               2  datesold     Num      8       8    MMDDYY8.
MMDDYY8.
               3  listprice    Num      8      16    DOLLAR9.2
DOLLAR9.2
               5  publisher    Char     8      32
               6  section      Char     8      40
               7  title        Char     8      48
                          -----Sort Information-----
                          Sortedby:        cost
                          Validated:       YES
                          Character Set: ANSI
```

The output shows that PROC CONTENTS gives a lot of information about the dataset just analyzed. For example, it gives the name of the dataset, the location, when it was created, the host that created the dataset, and the time of the last modification. It also provides the number of observations in the dataset, and the name, type, format, informat, length, and position of each variable.

As you can see from the example above, the only statement needed to run this procedure is proc contents and data = option. You can use out = option to create a dataset for the output. There are many options that can be used with this procedure. If you need any of them, please look at SAS online documentation or consult SAS procedure guide.

3.1.3 PROC SORT

This procedure sorts observations in a SAS dataset by one or more variables. It can store the result in a new dataset or replace the original.

Example 3.7
```
proc sort data=employee;
by name;
run;
```
This program sorts the dataset `employee` by name and replaces the data set by its sorted version.
See section 3.3 for more details on PROC SORT.

3.1.4 PROC COPY

This procedure copies a SAS data library or selected members of the library. You can also use this procedure to transport SAS datasets from one host to another.

Example 3.8
```
libname old 'c:\mydata';
libname new 'c:\tempdata';
proc copy in=old out=new;
run;
```
Upon the execution of this program all members in the SAS data library `old` will be copied to the library `new`.

3.1.5 PROC FORMAT

There are four different categories of formats in the SAS system:
1. Numeric
2. Character
3. Date and time
4. User-defined formats created with the FORMAT procedure
First let's look at the formats created by the FORMAT procedure. At the end of this section we will consider formats using format statements.

The FORMAT procedure defines output formats for labeling values and informats for reading data. You can use the FORMAT procedure to define your own informants and formats for character or numeric variables.

FORMATS

A word immediately followed by a period indicates a format name, for example `dollar.` or `dollar10.`. Formats are for *writing* (output) variable values.

Standard SAS formats write variable values in predefined ways. User-defined formats associate variable values with character values and can convert a value to a different form for output. For example, you can convert a numeric value to a character value or a character string to another character string.

The FORMAT procedure uses `value` and `invalue` to create two user defined formats. VALUE formats convert output values into a different form. For example, a numeric value may be changed to a character value, or a character string to another character string. A VALUE statement generates value formats; for example

```
value sex 1='male' 2='female';
Value grade 4='A' 3='B';
```

Notice the difference between the two following programs in `grade` as a variable name and `grade.` as a format, and the position of the $ sign.

Example 3.9
```
proc format;
value grade 4='A' 3='B';
data b;
input name $ grade ;
format grade grade.;
cards;
kim 4
din 3
john 4
;
run;
proc print ;
run;
```

Output:

```
          The SAS System        09:21 Friday, January 2,
          2004
                    Obs    name    grade
                    1      kim     A
                    2      din     B
                    3      john    A
```

Example 3.10
```
proc format;
invalue $grade 4='A' 3='B' 2='C' 1='D';
run;

data c;
input name $ grade $grade.;
```

```
cards;
ali 4
bob 3
jim 2
mike 1
kim 4
;
run;
proc print data=c;
run;
```

Output:

```
        The SAS System           09:21 Friday, January 2,
        2004
                     Obs     name     grade
                      1      ali        A
                      2      bob        B
                      3      jim        C
                      4      mike       D
```

INFORMAT

A word immediately followed by a period indicates an informat name. Informats are for *reading* (input) variable values. Standard SAS informats read variable values in a predefined way. User-defined informats convert a number to a character string, or a character string to a numeric value. User-defined informats read only character data values.

The FORMAT procedure uses `value` and `invalue` to create two user-defined informats. VALUE informats read variables and transform character values to numeric values, or one character string to a different character string. The INVALUE statement generates value informats.

Example 3.11
```
proc format;
invalue grade 'A'=4 'B'=3 'C'=2 'D'=1 'F' = 0;
run;

data grade;
input name $ (course1 - course4)(: grade.);
gpa = mean(of course1 - course4);
cards;
ali A B C D
bob B B C F
jim D F A A
mike C B B D
kim A A A A
```

```
;
run;
proc print data=grade;
run;
```

Output:

```
        The SAS System              20:37 Friday, January 2, 2004
    Obs     name    course1    course2    course3    course4
gpa
     1      ali        4          3          2          1
2.50
     2      bob        3          3          2          0
2.00
     3      jim        1          0          4          4
2.25
     4      mike       2          3          3          1
2.25
     5      kim        4          4          4          4
4.00
```

Note: When creating a SAS dataset, the FORMAT and INFORMAT statements used in a DATA step permanently associate the FORMAT or INFORMAT with a variable. When using the same statements in a PROC step, the FORMAT and INFORMAT statements associate the format with a variable for the duration of that step.

3.2 Using SAS procedures to investigate and evaluate the quality of data

The following procedures help you investigate the quality of data you are going to analyze.
1. PROC FREQ
2. PROC MEANS
3. PROC SUMMARY

3.2.1 PROC FREQ

PROC FREQ counts the number (frequency) of occurrences of each variable. To obtain different statistics from the data, use the FREQ procedure. This procedure can produce one-way to n-way frequency and cross-tabulation tables. You can also analyze relationships among variables. PROC FREQ produces printed output by default. PROC FREQ lists each variable value along with the frequencies and percentages. The following program demonstrates the simplest form of PROC FREQ and produces the output.

Example 3.12
```
libname a 'c:\mydata';
```

```
proc freq data= a.books;
run;
```

The output of this program is too long for our purposes to include here. To limit the output for only one variable and create a one-way frequency table we can add the TABLES statement:

```
libname a 'c:\mydata';
proc freq data= a.books;
tables cost;
run;
```

Output:

The SAS System	14:58 Monday, January 5, 2004			
		The FREQ Procedure		
Cumulative				Cumulative
Percent	cost	Frequency	Percent	Frequency
8.33	$10.25	1	8.33	1
25.00	$12.95	2	16.67	3
33.33	$15.99	1	8.33	4
41.67	$18.95	1	8.33	5
50.00	$19.95	1	8.33	6
58.33	$24.99	1	8.33	7
66.67	$31.95	1	8.33	8
75.00	$46.99	1	8.33	9
83.33	$51.50	1	8.33	10
91.67	$65.99	1	8.33	11
100.00	$99.99	1	8.33	12

To create two-way cross-tabulation tables, state the variable names separated by an asterisk.

Example 3.13
```
data b;
input name $ salary;
cards;
jon 45000
jane 66000
;run;
proc freq data=b;
tables name *salary;
run;
```

Output:

```
The SAS System          10:34 Tuesday, January 6, 2004
                                The FREQ Procedure
                                Table of name by salary
                        name        salary
                        Frequency,
                        Percent   ,
                        Row Pct   ,
                        Col Pct   ,   45000,    66000,   Total

                        jane      ,       0 ,       1 ,       1
                                  ,    0.00 ;   50.00 ;   50.00
                                  ,    0.00 ;  100.00 ,
                                  ,    0.00 ;  100.00 ,

                        jon       ,       1 ,       0 ,       1
                                  ,   50.00 ;    0.00 ;   50.00
                                  ,  100.00 ;    0.00 ,
                                  ,  100.00 ,    0.00 ,

                        Total             1         1         2
                                      50.00     50.00    100.00
```

Notice that the values of the variable mentioned in the TABLES statement can be either character or numeric.

If you want to create a three-way (or n-way) cross tabulation table, state the three (or n) variable names separated by asterisks in the TABLES statement. Multi-way tables generate a great amount of output. They may require thousands of pages, so be careful.

One last thing about PROC FREQ—although many other SAS procedures can produce frequency counts, PROC FREQ is distinguished by its ability to compute Chi-square tests and measures of association for two-way and n-way tables. This is how to add the Chi-square test to PROC FREQ:
Tables name*gender / chisq; where *name* and *gender* are two character variables in the dataset.

3.2.2 PROC MEANS

PROC MEANS produces statistics for numeric variables. PROC MEANS computes statistics for the entire SAS dataset or a subset of it and produces output by default. PROC MEANS and PROC SUMMARY are very similar procedures; however, PROC SUMMARY does not produce a printed output by default. The following is an example of the simplest use of PROC MEANS procedure.

Example 3.14
```
libname a 'c:\mydata';
proc means data=a.books;
run;
```

Output from Example 3.14:

```
The SAS System        10:46 Wednesday, January 7, 2004    1
                                    The MEANS Procedure
Variable    N          Mean        Std Dev        Minimum
Maximum

cost        9      25.9466667    14.7143518     10.2500000
51.5000000
datesold    9      14063.89     129.4656754     13880.00
14225.00
listprice   9      22.4966667    13.2760367      8.0000000
45.9900000
```

The following statements control the MEANS procedure:

VAR, CLASS, BY, OUTPUT, FREQ, WEIGHT, ID.

Let's look at some illustrations of the use these statements.

VAR statement

Example 3.15
```
libname a 'c:\mydata';
proc means data=a.books;
var listprice;
run;
```

Output:

```
The SAS System        09:40 Thursday, January 8, 2004
                         The MEANS Procedure
                      Analysis Variable : listprice
N         Mean        Std Dev       Minimum        Maximum

9     22.4966667    13.2760367     8.0000000    45.9900000
```

If no specific statistics are requested, PROC MEANS prints the name of the variable, N, MEAN, STD, MIN, and MAX. To get a specific statistic you must state it in the PROC MEANS statement. In the following example the statistic MIN is requested.

Example 3.16
```
libname a 'c:\mydata';
```

```
proc means data=a.books min;
var listprice;
run;
```

Output:

```
The SAS System          09:40 Thursday, January 8, 2004
                                  The MEANS Procedure
                            Analysis Variable : listprice
                                       Minimum

                                    8.0000000
```

CLASS statement

CLASS variables can be either numeric or character. The CLASS statement assigns variables used to form subgroups. CLASS variables normally have a small number of values.

Example 3.17 In the following example, to keep the output short, I requested calculation only of the statistic MAXIMUM.

```
libname a 'c:\mydata';
proc means data=a.books max;
class listprice;
run;
```

Output:

```
The SAS System        09:40 Thursday, January 8, 2004
                                 The MEANS Procedure
                          N
              listprice  Obs    Variable      Maximum

                  $8.00   1     cost        10.2500000
                                datesold      14036.00
                 $10.55   1     cost        12.9500000
                                datesold      13880.00
                 $11.95   1     cost        15.9900000
                                datesold      13881.00
                 $15.99   1     cost        18.9500000
                                datesold      14094.00
                 $19.50   1     cost        24.9900000
                                datesold      14130.00
                 $21.99   1     cost        19.9500000
                                datesold      13973.00
                 $28.50   1     cost        31.9500000
                                datesold      14162.00
                 $40.00   1     cost        46.9900000
                                datesold      14194.00
                 $45.99   1     cost        51.5000000
                                datesold      14225.00
```

BY statement

If you have a large dataset, it is a good idea to use the BY statement to subdivide your data. When you use the BY statement, your data must be sorted according to the BY variables. A BY statement is used to produce separate analysis on observations in groups defined by the BY variables. With large datasets, a BY statement is preferable since PROC MEANS does not need to hold all the groups in memory.

Example 3.18
```
libname a 'c:\mydata';
proc means data=a.books max;
by listprice;
run;
```

Output:

```
The SAS System          09:40 Thursday, January 8, 2004   7
--------------------------------------- listprice=$8.00 ------------------
                                   The MEANS Procedure
                             Variable          Maximum

                             cost           10.2500000
                             datesold       14036.00
------------------------------------------ listprice=$10.55 ------------------
                             Variable          Maximum

                             cost           12.9500000
                             datesold       13880.00
------------------------------------------ listprice=$11.95 ------------------
                             Variable          Maximum

                             cost           15.9900000
                             datesold       13881.00
------------------------------------------ listprice=$15.99 ------------------
                             Variable          Maximum

                             cost           18.9500000
                             datesold       14094.00
```

OUTPUT statement

You can use as many OUTPUT statements as you wish with PROC MEANS.

Example 3.19
```
libname a 'c:\mydata';
proc means data=a.books ;
```

```
output out=newbook;
run;
```

Output:

```
The SAS System        10:26 Monday, January 12, 2004  2
Obs    _TYPE_    _FREQ_    _STAT_        cost      datesold    listprice
1        0        9        N            $9.00     01/10/60      $9.00
2        0        9        MIN         $10.25     01/01/98      $8.00
3        0        9        MAX         $51.50     12/12/98     $45.99
4        0        9        MEAN        $25.95     07/03/98     $22.50
```

In the following example the output dataset `new_cost` contains the mean of the variable `cost`. You can use this dataset to perform further analysis of your data.

Example 3.20
```
libname a 'c:\mydata';
proc means data=a.books mean;
var cost;
output out=new_cost    mean=cost_mean;
run;
```

Output:

```
The SAS System       14:54 Tuesday, February 15, 2005
                                 The MEANS Procedure
                                 Analysis Variable : cost
                                           Mean

                                 25.9466667
```

The following example shows how to calculate the percentage of cost of each book in terms of the mean cost of all books.

Example 3.21
```
data a;
set a.books;
if _n_=1 then set new_cost;
perc_cost=(cost/cost_mean)*100;
run;
proc print data=a(keep=cost perc_cost);
run;
```

Output:

```
The SAS System       14:54 Tuesday, February 15, 2005
                                                      perc_
                          Obs        cost             cost
                          1         $10.25           39.504
                          2         $12.95           49.910
                          3         $15.99           61.626
                          4         $18.95           73.034
                          5         $19.95           76.888
                          6         $24.99           96.313
                          7         $31.95          123.137
                          8         $46.99          181.102
                          9         $51.50          198.484
```

Below you will find the printout of dataset books, in case you would like to see more detail.

```
proc print data=a.books;
run;
```

Output:

```
The SAS System     14:54 Tuesday, February 15, 2005   12
Obs        cost    datesold   listprice   author    publisher
section
1         $10.25   06/06/98    $8.00      parviz    barns
science
2         $12.95   01/01/98    $10.55     mohamad   barnes
science
3         $15.99   01/02/98    $11.95     davood    borders    art
4         $18.95   08/03/98    $15.99     barbara   oxford
cooking
5         $19.95   04/04/98    $21.99     daryoosh  borders    art
6         $24.99   09/08/98    $19.50     hacib     oxford
cooking
7         $31.95   10/10/98    $28.50     mamal     oxford     art
8         $46.99   11/11/98    $40.00     reza      mcgraw
science
9         $51.50   12/12/98    $45.99     diba      barns      art
```

3.2.3 PROC SUMMARY

PROC SUMMARY produces summary statistics for numeric variables in a SAS dataset and outputs the result to a new SAS dataset. PROC SUMMARY performs tasks similar to those of PROC MEANS, but PROC SUMMARY does not produce a printed output by default.

PROC SUMMARY is controlled by the following statements: VAR, CLASS, BY, OUTPUT, FREQ, ID, WEIGHT.

If you omit the VAR statement with PROC SUMMARY, the output will consist of the count of observations.

Example 3.22
```
libname a 'c:\mydata';
proc summary data=a.books;
output out=nsum;
run;
proc print data=nsum;
run;
```

Output of this program is just one line stating the number of observations in the output dataset, 9, as shown below:

Output :

```
The SAS System        10:26 Monday, January 12, 2004
                   Obs    _TYPE_    _FREQ_
                   1        0         9
```

3.3 Sorting observations in a SAS dataset

PROC SORT is controlled by PROC SORT and BY statements. The BY statement is required.

PROC SORT sorts a SAS dataset by one or more variables, storing the result in a new SAS data set or replacing the original dataset.

Data are sorted by PROC SORT so that other SAS procedures can process the data in subsets using the BY statements. Data must be sorted before they can be match–merged, or updated. If you have an appropriate index for a dataset, the dataset need not be sorted in order to use a BY statement in a DATA or PROC step.

PROC SORT rearranges data in an ascending order by default. Suppose that you want to sort your data by one variable (the variable must appear in the BY statement). PROC SORT arranges data in such a way that observations with the lowest values will appear first, followed by observations with the second lowest values, and so on.

When sorting data by two or more variables, PROC SROT first rearranges data in the order of the first BY variable. Then it arranges the observations having the lowest value of the first variable in the order of the second variable. For example, if you sort a dataset containing state and city, PROC SORT first arranges the data so that Alabama's observations are first, then Alaska's, and so on. Then it arranges Alabama's observations by city so that Birmingham's observations are followed by Dalton's, and so on.

3.3.1 Sorting orders

When using PROC SORT, sorting order for numeric values as follows:
1. Missing (shown by a period or any special missing value)
2. Negative
3. Zero
4. Positive values.

Character values are sorted by using either the EBCDIC (extended binary-coded decimal interchange code) or the ASCII (American Standard Code For Information Interchange) collating sequence. In EBCDIC sequence, the lowercase letters are smaller than the uppercase ones and uppercase letters are smaller than digits. The blank is the smallest display character.

In order to sort in descending order, use the word *descending* as follows:
```
proc sort data=employee;
by descending salary;
run;
```

3.3.2 BY statement

Any number of variables can be specified in the BY statement. A BY statement must accompany PROC SORT; otherwise a syntax error results.

PROC SORT sorts data by the values of the variables mentioned in the BY statement.

Use the option DESCENDING in the BY statement to sort data in descending order.

3.3.3 Other options

OUTPUT

If an out= option appears in the sort statement, then a new data set containing the sorted data is produced. Otherwise, the original dataset will be replaced by the sorted one.

If you want to store the sorted data into a new SAS dataset, you will need to add out= option as follows:

```
proc sort data=employee out=newemp;
by name;
run;
```

You can sort a compressed dataset in much the same way as you would any other one. The resulting dataset will be compressed. If you specify an out=option the new dataset will not be compressed, unless you mention the option compress = yes.

Two important options of PROC SORT are nodup and nodupkey. Using these options, you can eliminate duplicated observation from a SAS dataset.

Nodup

Using this option, SAS eliminates all repeated observations, which have exactly the same value for every variable.

Example 3.23
```
data a;
input id name $ salary bonus;
cards;
1 smith 59000 4500
2 jordan 68000 6000
1 smith 59000 4500
;
run;
proc sort data=a nodup out=b;
by id;
run;
proc print data=b;
run;
```

Output:

```
The SAS System          08:55 Sunday, February 20, 2005
                    Obs     id      name      salary    bonus
                     1       1      smith     59000     4500
                     2       2      jordan    68000     6000
SAS prints a note in the Log informing you of the action taken.
NOTE: 1 duplicate observations were deleted.
NOTE: There were 3 observations read from the data set WORK.A.
NOTE: The data set WORK.B has 2 observations and 4 variables.
NOTE: PROCEDURE SORT used:
      real time              0.21 seconds
```

Nodupkey

This option deletes the observations that have the same value for the variable mentioned in the BY statement, here *id*.

Example 3.24
```
data a;
input id name $ salary bonus;
cards;
1 smith 59000 4500
1 jordan 68000 6000
3 woods 88000 7250
;
run;
proc sort data=a nodupkey out=c;
by id;
run;
proc print data=c;
run;
```

Output:

```
The SAS System        08:55 Sunday, February 20, 2005
                  Obs   id    name    salary     bonus
                   1    1     smith   59000      4500
                   2    3     woods   88000      7250
```

3.4 Modifying variable attributes using options and statements in the DATA step

Dataset options are those that appear in parentheses after the SAS dataset name. These options apply only to the dataset with which they appear. Some of these options are
1. Renaming
2. Specifying variables to be included or dropped in later processing
3. Selecting only the first or last n observations for the DATA statement

Output options in the DATA step may appear in the DATA statement, but not in the output statement. Some of the most used options are compress = , drop = , keep = , obs = , rename = , where = . *Note:* All options must be followed by an equal sign.

Example 3.25
```
data c( keep=name tax);
input name $ salary;
tax = salary*.08;
if salary lt 10000 then tax=0;
else tax= salary*.08;
cards;
james 13000
moj 27000
bahman 6004
karl 999990
;
run;
proc print data=c;
title 'IT IS TAX SEASON';
run;
```

Output:

```
          IT IS TAX SEASON          12:22 Sunday, January 18, 2004   12
                                            Obs      name
                                             1       james
                                             2       moj
                                             3       bahman
                                             4       karl
```

Notice the two equal signs used in the following rename option.
```
data d;
set c(rename=(name=firstnam));
run;

proc print data=d;
title 'name changed to first name';
run;
```

Output:

```
          name changed to first name

          11:14 Monday, January 19, 2004

          tax                             Obs      firstnamt

          1040.0                           1       james

          2160.0                           2       moj

          0.0                              3       bahman

                                           4       karl
```

The option `compress=` is meaningful only when you are creating a new SAS data set.

Suppose that we have two data sets `a` and `b` and we want to merge them using data set options. This is how we procede:

```
Merge a (where = (sales gt 12000 ) b (where = (region = 'east'
)) ;
```

Notice if instead of WHERE you use IF; then an error results with no output.

Any variable in the SAS system has the following attributes:

1. Name
2. Type
3. Length
4. Informat
5. Format
6. Label.
    Let's look at these attributes one by one.

1. *Name.* A SAS variable name can be up to 32 characters long, and it must begin with a letter or an underscore. Other characters can be letters, digits, or underscores. Blanks are not allowed.

2. *Type.* A variable is of type character or numeric. The type is assumed by the SAS system to be numeric unless it is indicated as a character. If the type of a variable is not explicitly defined, then its type is defined by its first appearance.

If a character value is assigned to a numeric variable, SAS attempts to convert it. If SAS is unable to do the conversion, an error message will be sent to the log and a missing value (a dot) to the output.

3. *Length.* The length of a variable is the number of bytes allocated by SAS in order to store the value of the variable. The length of a numeric variable affects only the output of that variable, but the length of a character variable affects both input and output. The length of a variable, appearing initially on the left side of an equality sign, assumes the length of the variable on the right side of the equality sign. If length of a variable is not explicitly defined, this property is defined by the initial appearance.

4. *Informat.* It is this instruction that SAS uses to read data values. If you do not specify an informat for a variable, the default for a numeric variable is `w.`, and for a character is `$w.`.

5. *Format.* This attribute provides instruction to the SAS system to print the variable values. If you do not specify a format for a variable, the default for a numeric variable is `w.`, and for a character, `$w.`.

6. *Label.* This attribute gives descriptive information for a variable and is good for report writing. Use a LABEL statement to assign a label to a variable.

3.5 Conditionally executing SAS statements

The conditional statement causes the DATA step to continue processing those raw data records or observations from a SAS dataset that meet the condition(s) specified in the conditional statement(s). Therefore, the resulting SAS data set is a subset of the original dataset. The conditional statements are

1. WHERE

2. IF , IF – THEN / ELSE

3. SELECT.

3.5.1 Where statement and comparison with IF statement

If you want to improve the efficiency of your program, use a WHERE statement. This statement does not require the SAS system to read all observations in the input dataset.

The WHERE statement gives you the ability to specify a condition that the data must satisfy *before* the SAS system brings the observations from a SAS dataset into a program data vector.

You can use WHERE with any SAS procedure that can read a SAS dataset.

Example 3.26
```
libname a 'c:\mydata';
data b;
set a.books;
where cost lt 12.90;
run;
proc print data=b;
run;
```

Output:

```
The SAS System          17:35 Sunday, February 1, 2004
Obs    cost    datesold    listprice    author    publisher    section title
 1    $10.25   06/06/98       $8.00     parviz      barns       science maths
```

The following program produces the same output:

```
libname a 'c:\mydata';
data b;
set a.books( where=( cost lt 10.95));
run;
```

Notice the equal sign after `where`. If you omit it, an error results with no output.

You use the WHERE statement in the SET, MERGE, and UPDATE statements in a SAS DATA step. The variables in a WHERE statement must exist in the dataset. You cannot use a WHERE statement with programming statements that select observations by observation number, such as OBS = . When you use the WHERE, statement the value of FIRSTOBS must be (1).

(*Note:* You cannot use a WHERE statement to select records from an external file containing raw data. Also, you can't use the WHERE statement as part of an IF–THEN statement or any other conditional statement.)

The WHERE statement has priority over a BY statement; in a DATA step , this means that if both WHERE and BY statements exist, the WHERE statement is executed before BY groups are created.

Operands used in WHERE expressions

You can use different operands with the WHERE expression. In Example 3.27 you will see some of these operands. Before we look at examples, notice that you can't use variables created in the DATA step in a WHERE expression since the WHERE statement is executed before SAS brings observations into the DATA step or PROC step.

Example 3.27
```
where grade > 69;
where date >= '29feb99'd ;
where date >= '31dec99' d and time >='11:59't;
where state = 'georgia';
where state in ('nj' , 'ny', 'fl' );
where id in (3 5 7 9);
where id in (3,5,7,9);
```

Notice the presence of "d" and "t" for date and time respectively.
You can use a numeric variable on its own (without "d", or "t") in a WHERE statement. If the value of a variable is missing or zero, the SAS system considers it to be false; the SAS system will interpret any other value to be true. For example, the variables "empnumb" and "ssn" of each employee are used as follows in a WHERE expression:
```
Where empnumb ;
Where ssn;
```

You can also use a character variable on its own in a WHERE expression. If the value of the variable is not blank, the SAS system selects that observation.

(*Note:* You can't use SAS functions in WHERE expressions.)

Operators used in WHERE expressions

The following operators are valid *only* for the WHERE expression.
1.   BETWEEN–AND

2. CONTAINS
3. IS NULL or IS MISSING
4. LIKE
5. SOUNDS–LIKE

Example 3.28
where empnum between 1000 and 9999;
where compname contains 'soft';
where ssn is missing;
where ssn is null;
where name is not missing;
where lsname like 'K%';
where name =*'smith';

Note: You can use the NOT operator with the IS MISSING or the IS NULL operators.

The LIKE operator distinguishes between uppercase and lowercase characters. In the statement `where lsname like 'K%';`, the WHERE statement selects all names that begin with the letter K. The name can be of any length. Use one underscore in a pattern to match one character in the value for each underscore character. More than one underscore may be used.

For example `Like 'j_hn'` gives either `john` or `jahn`.
or
`Like 'j_hn_'` gives `johni` or `johne`.

You can combine the NOT operator with the LIKE operator.

The SOUNDS-LIKE operator uses `=*` with character variables that have different spellings of the same word. For example, if you want to select observations that have names that sound like Smith from the list containing Smythe, Schmit, or Smitt, use the statement `where name = *'smith';` which contains an operator similar to the one in last line of the example presented above.

IF statement

An IF statement is used to select records from raw data or observations from a SAS dataset that meet a specific condition. The result is a subset of the original external file or SAS dataset. If the expression is valid for the observation or record, the SAS system continues executing statements in the DATA step. Otherwise no further statements are processed for that observation or record.

Example 3.29
```
libname a 'c:\mydata';
data b;
set a.books;
```

```
if cost=10.25;
run;
proc print data=b;
run;
```

The result is a dataset, which includes only those books that cost exactly $10.95.

Output:

```
    The SAS System      11:14 Wednesday, February 18, 2004
 Obs    cost    datesold    listprice    author   publisher    section
 title
  1    $10.25   06/06/98       $8.00     parviz     barns      science
 maths
```

The following statement processes the observations for which the value of the variable cost is not missing or is not zero.
If cost;

The IF statement is equivalent to the following IF-THEN statement:
`If not(expression) then delete;` expression is any valid SAS expression.

Comparison between IF and WHERE statements

The IF and WHERE statements are not equivalent. The most important differences are :
1. The WHERE statement is more efficient than the IF statement because WHERE selects observations before they are brought into the program data vector.
2. WHERE selects observations only from a SAS dataset. The IF statement can select observations from a SAS dataset or from a raw dataset.
3. The IF statement is executable while the WHERE statement is not.
4. If you use the IF statement in a DATA step, you can include SAS functions. You cannot do the same with the WHERE statement.
5. You cannot use the IF statement in a PROC step.

3.5.2 IF-THEN/ELSE statement

The IF-THEN statement selects observations from a SAS dataset or records from an external file that meet the condition specified in the IF clause. The ELSE statement is optional in case the THEN clause is not executed.

Example 3.30
```
libname a 'c:\mydata';
data c;
set a.books;
if cost=10.25 then delete;
run;
proc print data=c;
```

```
run;
```

Output: The output dataset will not contain the observations where the cost is $10.25.

```
The SAS System          10:45 Sunday, July 25, 2004
cost     datesold    listprice    author     publisher    section    title
$12.95   01/01/98      $10.55     mohamad     barnes       science
algebra
$15.99   01/02/98      $11.95     davood      borders      art        music
$18.95   08/03/98      $15.99     barbara     oxford       cooking
pastery
$19.95   04/04/98      $21.99     daryoosh    borders      art
guitar
$24.99   09/08/98      $19.50     hacib       oxford       cooking
bagels
$31.95   10/10/98      $28.50     mamal       oxford       art
manageme
```

The following program is a very efficient way of using the IF-THEN/ELSE statement:

```
libname a 'c:\mydata';
data c;
set a.books;
if cost le 10.25 then group=1;
else if cost gt 10.25 and cost lt 19.99 then group=2;
else if cost gt 20 then group=3;
run;
```

3.5.3 SELECT statement

SELECT is an efficient alternative to the IF-THEN/ELSE statement. The SELECT statement allows the SAS system to execute the selection of one of several statements. You must have at least one WHEN statement in a SELECT group. You can use an optional OTHERWISE statement in case none of the WHEN conditions are met. To finish a SELECT group, you must use an END statement.

Example 3.31
```
Select ( C ) ;
when ( 1 )  tax = sal*.12;
when ( 2 ) tax = sal*.18;
when (3, 4 ) tax = sal*28;
otherwise;
end;
```

If more than one WHEN expression is valid, the SAS systems uses the first one only. When a large number of conditions must be checked, the SELECT statement is more efficient than the IF THEN / ELSE statement.

3.6 Using assignment statements in the DATA step

When a variable is mentioned for the first time on the left side of an assignment statement, it is assigned the same type as in the value on the right side.

If a variable appears for the first time on the right side of an assignment with no prior value assigned, the SAS system assumes its type to be numeric and its value to be missing. A note will be printed in the log saying that the variable is not initialized:
```
score = score +1;
```
The *score* has not yet been given an initial value. You can use a RETAIN statement to initialize the value of the variable *score*. In the example bellow, *score* has been initialized to 1 and in the second statement *score* has been updated by one:
```
Retain score 1;
score = score + 1;
```
Instead of the these two lines, we can use the following line:
```
Score + 1;
```
Notice that no equal sign has been used. This summation statement initializes the value of *score* to zero and keeps the previous value of *score* for the new observation.

A subsequent LENGTH statement can change the length of a numeric variable but not that of a character variable. The LENGTH statement specifies the number of bytes used to store the value of a variable. Valid variable lengths depend on the host system. LENGTH is not an executable statement. The statement:
```
Length name $ 20.;
```
assigns the length of the variable *name* to 20.

The following length statement sets the length of the character variable name to 20 and changes the default number of bytes used for storing the values of the newly created character value from 8 to 4:
```
Length name $ 20. default = 4;
```

3.7 Accumulating sub-totals and totals using DATA step statements

To accumulate numeric variable values, use a sum statement or a sum function.

3.7.1 SUM statement

The SUM statement adds the value of a numeric variable to an accumulator.

Remember that the value of a variable is set to zero before the SAS system reads the first observation. SAS stores the variable's value from one iteration to the next. If you want the first value of your variable to be different from zero, you must include it in a RETAIN statement.

Example 3.32
```
input x y;
sum + x;
cards;
1 2
3 4
5 6
```

```
;
run;
proc print data=a;
run;
```

Output:

```
The SAS System      12:19 Thursday, February 26, 2004      1
                              Obs      x      y      sum
                               1       1      2       1
                               2       3      4       4
                               3       5      6       9
```

TIP: Inserting the line `sum = 0;` *after the input statement results in resetting* `sum` *to zero before updating it with the x value:*
```
input x y;
sum = 0;
sum + x;
```
   Putting `sum = 0;` *after the line* `sum + x;` *results in the value of* `sum` *being zero for each output.*
```
Input x y;
Sum + x;
Sum = 0;
```
   Putting `sum = 0;` *right before the line* `run;` *results in an error–not a syntax error.*

TIP: In the next example a new variable `z` *is introduced, and its initial value is blank. But the result was the same as Example 3.32. SAS went to the next line and picked up the first value and assigned it to* `z`, *ignoring the remaining values on the second line. SAS then went to the third line of data and continued as follows:*

Example 3.33
```
data a;
input x y z;
sum = x + y + z ;
cards;
1 2
3 4 5
6 7 8
;
run;
```

Output:

```
         The SAS System      12:19 Thursday, February 26, 2004
                           Obs    x    y    z    sum

                            1     1    2    3      6
                            2     6    7    8     21
```

Inserting a dot (.) as the value of z on the first line results in the value of sum also being a dot. Adding a slash (\ ) for the value of z on the first line results in the same output as placing a dot for z on first line. The SUM statement is equivalent to using the SUM function and RETAIN statement.

3.7.2 SUM function

The SUM function returns the sum of non-missing values. All arguments used in the SUM function must be numeric.
```
A = sum (1,2,3,4);
B = sum (x, y, z );
```

TIP: The statement AA = sum (1 + 2 + 3); gives a syntax error. You can use an of before your variables such as:
```
C = sum ( of x1 - x3); or
D = sum ( of x1 - x3 , 5);
```

TIP: The statements DD = sum (x + y +) ; and DD = sum(x + y -) ; gave syntax errors. The statement DD = sum (- x + y) ; causes SAS to change the sign of x and add it to the value of y and assign the result to sum. The statement DD = sum (x + y + .) ; results in the value of DD to be missing (.) in each output and gives a note in the log stating that the missing value was generated as a result of an operation on missing values.

3.8 Using SAS functions to manipulate character data, numeric data, and SAS date values

A SAS function returns the value of a computation that needs zero or more arguments. The arguments must be enclosed in parentheses. Arguments can be constants, names, or expressions that may include other functions.

SAS function arguments must be preceded by the word of or must be separated by commas. Parentheses must always be supplied even if no argument is needed. SAS functions can be used in both DATA step and in procedure programming.

We will consider the following SAS functions:
1.   MAX
2.   MIN
3.   MEAN
4.   SUM

5. PUT
6. COMPRESS
7. LEFT
8. TRIM
9. DATE
10. DAY
11. SUBSTR

1. MAX. The MAX function needs at least two numeric arguments; it returns the largest value of the arguments.

Example 3.34
```
data a;
y=max(1,2,3);
yy=max(1,2,3,.);
input x1 x2 x3;
yyy=max(of x1-x3);
cards;
1 2 3
;
run;
proc print data=a(drop=x1 x2 x3);
run;
```

Output:

```
             The SAS System        08:41 Monday, February 21, 2005

                          Obs      y      yy     yyy
                           1       3      3       3
```

Each of these returns the number 3.

2. MIN. The MIN function needs at least two numeric arguments and returns the smallest value of the arguments.
```
minsal = min ( 1, 2, 3 );
minsal = min(1, 2, 3, . );
minsal = min ( of sal1 - sal3 ); where sal1 =1 , sal2 = 2, sal3
= 3.
```
Each of these returns the value 1.

3. MEAN. The MEAN function requires at least one numeric argument and returns the mean of the arguments.
```
avgnum = mean (1, 2, 3 );
avgnum = mean (1, 2, 3, . );
avgnum ( of x1 - x3 );
where x1 = 1, x2 = 2, x3 = 3.
```

4. SUM. The SUM function requires at least two numeric arguments and returns the mean of the arguments. The arguments are numeric. At least two arguments are required. It returns the sum of arguments.

```
A = sum (10, 20 ,30 );
B = sum ( 10, 20, 30, . );
C = sum ( of x1 - x3 );
Where x1 = 10, x2 = 20, x3 = 30.
```

Each one of these functions returns the value 60.

5. PUT. You can use the PUT function to write the value of a character variable with a specific format or to onvert a numeric value to a character value. The PUT function gives the result as an output, while the PUT statement returns its result in the log. The PUT function takes the form of `new_var = put(variable , format)`.

6. COMPRESS. This function removes blanks or characters from a character expression. In following example, it removes all blanks:

Example 3.35
```
data b;
name = 'Dog lass';
actualname=compress(name);
run;
proc print data=b;
run;
```

Output:

```
The SAS System            20:07 Monday, August 23, 2004
                          Obs        name       actualname
                           1       Dog lass      Doglass
```

7. LEFT. The LEFT function removes the blanks from the beginning of a character string and puts them at the end of the same string. The length of the value remains unchanged:
```
title = '   This year tax'
newtitle = left(title);
```
The new variable `newtitle` will not have the blank at the beginning.

8. TRIM. The TRIM function removes blanks at the end of an argument. It is useful for concatenating.

9. DATE. The DATE function returns the value of today's date as the number of days from January 1, 1960. For example, today's date (2-29-04) will be represented as 16130.
```
Data a;
Today = date();
Run;
```

The alias for the DATE function is TODAY.

10. DAY. This function returns an integer as the number of the day of the month. For example, today's (2-29-04) DAY value is 29:
```
data c;
FD = '29feb04'd;
today = day(FD);
run;
```

TIP: Do not forget the letter d after the date. If this is omitted, you will receive a note in the log and a missing value (a period) for today in the output.

11. SUBSTR. The SUBSTR function has two operations depending on which side of the assignment statement it is placed:
a. If you place it on the right side of an assignment statement, SUBSTR returns a portion of an expression that is specified in its argument. The arguments of SUBSTR also contain the position where the string starts, and can also contain the number of characters in the substring:
```
data c;
d = '29feb04';
month = substr(d,3,3);
year = substr(d,6,2);
run;
```

The output for month will be feb and for year 04.

TIP: If you do not specify the second number in the argument of SUBSTR, the SAS system gives you the string from the specified position to the end.Month = substr(d,3); assigns the value of feb 04 to month.

b. If you place the SUBSTR function on the left side of an assignment statement, the SAS system places the value of the expression on the right side of the assignment statement into the argument of the SUSTR, replacing the n characters starting with the character specified in the second position.

Example 3.36
```
data c;
a = 'subjectively';;
substr(a,4)='sandwich';
put a;
run;
proc print data=c;
run;
```

Output:

```
                The SAS System      08:41 Monday, February 21, 2005
                                    Obs         a
                                    1      subsandwich
```

12. INDEX. The INDEX function searches a source from left to right for a specific character string and returns the position of the first character of the string. If it cannot find the string requested, it returns the value of 0.

Example 3.37
```
data d;
a = 'total';;
m = 't';
x = index(a,m);
put x;
run;

proc print data=d;
run;
```

Output:

```
                    The SAS System      08:41 Monday, February 21, 2005
                                        Obs      a       m    x
                                        1      total     t    1
```

Notice in the next program that the value of x is zero, since the function can't find q.
```
data ed;
a = 'total';;
m = 'q';
x = index(a,m);
put x;
run;
proc print data=ed;
run;
```

Output:

```
                    The SAS System      08:41 Monday, February 21, 2005
                                        Obs       a      m    x
                                        1       total    q    0
```

3.9 Using SAS functions to convert character data to numeric data and vice versa

To convert the type of SAS data values, we use. The INPUT function to convert character data values to numeric ones and the PUT function to convert numeric data values to character values (Section 3.8, paragraph 5).

Use the INPUT function to convert a character value to a numeric value. This function enables you to read the value of a source using a specific informat, which determines the type of the result.

Example 3.38
```
data t;
input sale $9.;
y = input(sale,comma9.);
cards;
122,000
;
run;
```

Output:

```
            The SAS System        10:26 Monday, March 1, 2004
                                Obs      sale       y
                                 1     122,000   122000
```

TIP: *When changing* 122,000 *to* 12.20, -122000, *or* +122000, *the SAS system accepted the values of* sale *as numeric and gave* 12.2, -122000, +122000 *in the output, respectively Deleting $ in the INPUT line caused the SAS system to give a note in the log saying:* Invalid data for sale, _Error_ = 1. *The output was a missing value for* sale *and a missing value for* y.

Deleting the dot (.) after 9 *in the INPUT line and keeping* $, *resulted in no message in the log, and no value was given for* sale *and the value for* y *was a missing value.*

3.10 Processing data using DO loops

If you want to process a group of statements, use the DO statement. We will look at the following DO statements for group processing:
1. DO
2. Iterative DO

3. DO UNTIL
4. DO WHILE

3.10.1 DO

We start with the simplest DO group processing, which is the DO statement. To end group processing, you need an END statement. The statements included between the DO and the END statements are called a "DO group". The DO statement is usually used within an IF–THEN/ELSE statement.

Example 3.39
```
libname a 'c:\mydata';
data tax;
set a.books;
if listprice le 19.99 then do;
taxrate=.07;
end;
else taxrate = .09;
tax = listprice*taxrate;
run;
```

Output:

```
cost    datesold  listprice author   publisher section   title   taxrate tax
$10.25  06/06/98  $8.00     parviz   barns     science   maths   0.07    0.5600
$12.95  01/01/98  $10.55    mohamad  barnes    science   algebra 0.07    0.7385
$15.99  01/02/98  $11.95    davood   borders   art       music   0.07    0.836
$18.95  08/03/98  $15.99    barbara  oxford    cooking   pastery 0.07    1.119
$19.95  04/04/98  $21.99    daryoosh borders   art       guitar  0.09    .9791
$24.99  09/08/98  $19.50    hacib    oxford    cooking   bagels  0.07    1.3650
$31.95  10/10/98  $28.50    mamal    oxford    art       manageme0.09    2.5650
$46.99  11/11/98  $40.00    reza     mcgraw    science   fortran 0.09    3.6000
```

Notice the place of the END statement; it is before the ELSE statement. If the END and ELSE statement change places, an error message is given with no output.

3.10.2 Iterative DO

Iterative DO executes until a matching END is encountered. The execution is based on the value of an index variable. This DO statement can contain UNTIL or WHILE clauses. The following are examples of iterative DO:

```
do i = 1 to 10;
do i = 10;
do month = 'jan', 'feb', 'mar';
do count = 10, 100, 1000;
```

```
do i = 1 to 10 by 2;
```

Notice that the order of the TO and BY statements can be reversed. The value of the BY increment is evaluated prior to execution of the loop. Any changes to the increment within the DO group do not affect the number of iterations.

In the following statement after execution, the value of count is 20:

```
do count = 2 to 18 by 2;
```

TIP: In the previous statement, if you start the value of count with 1 and increment by 2, the last value of i will be 19.

The output of the following example is only one line, the final value of y.

Example 3.40
```
data b;
do i = 2 to 18 by 2;
y = i + 1;
end;
run;
```

If you want to include every value of y in the output, insert an OUTPUT statement before the END statement.

```
data b;
do i = 2 to 18 by 2;
y = i + 1;
output;
end;
run;
```

If no increment value is specified, the index variable is increased by one. Any attempt to jump out of the DO loop before the number of iterations have been completed will be ignored.

Modifications in the index variable within the DO loop may result in an infinite loop. The following two programs produced no output:
```
data b;
do i = 1 to 18 by -2;
y = i + 1;
output;
end;
run;
```

```
data b;
do i = 11 to 1 by 3;
y = i + 1;
output;
end;
```

```
run;
```

When the value of the increment is positive, the start(initial) value must be lower than the stop(final) value. On the other hand, if the value of the increment is negative, the start value must be higher than the stop value.

Notice in the first program that the last value of the index variable 'i' is –1, not +1, since the value of the index variable is decided prior to execution of the DO loop.

When you use UNTIL and WHILE clauses in the iterative DO, the value of the WHILE expression is evaluated *before* execution of each iteration of the DO loop. The value of the UNTIL expression is evaluated *after* execution of each iteration of the DO loop.

Example 3.41
```
data c;
x = 4;
do i = 1 to 10 while(x>y);
y = i + 1;
output;
end;
run;
```

Output:

```
                The SAS System           13:05 Monday, March 8, 2004
                          Obs    x    i    y
                           1     4    1    2
                           2     4    2    3
                           3     4    3    4
```

TIP: In the previous example, if you put the line x = 4; inside the DO loop, no observation will be produced, since the SAS system needs to know the value of x prior to execution of each iteration of the DO loop.

Let's use UNTIL and see what the result will be:
```
data c;
x = 4;
do i = 1 to 10 until(x<y);
y = i + 1;
output;
end;
run;
```

Output:

```
            The SAS System           13:05 Monday, March 8, 2004
                      Obs    x    i    y
                       1     4    1    2
                       2     4    2    3
                       3     4    3    4
                       4     4    4    5
```

TIP: Notice how the relation between x and y has changed from x < y to x > y. Compare the last value of y (=5) in the last program to the last value of y (=4) in the previous program. This difference is due to the fact that the value of y is evaluated after the execution of the DO loop.

3.10.3 DO UNTIL

This DO loop continues executing a group of statements until a condition is satisfied.

Example 3.42
```
data a;
n=0;
do until(n>=5);
n+1;
put n;
end;
run;
```

When n is 5, the loop is not executed. The output of this program is only one line, which gives the value of n equal to 5.

DO UNTIL checks the condition at the bottom of the loop.

TIP: Under the following conditions you may get into an infinite loop:
1. Deleting the statement n + 1; in the body of the loop
2. Inserting the line n = 0; inside the loop
Notice in the first case that by deleting the line n+1; you are creating a permanent condition. The value of n will always be zero. The same argument holds in the case(n = 0). In the program presented above also notice that if the condition n >= 5 is changed to n> 5, the value of n in the output and in the log will be 6 instead of 5 because the value of n is increased at the bottom of the loop and the condition is checked; the value of n is 6 so the loop stops executing. If on the last program, the value of n is changed from zero to a number larger than 5, the loop executes only once, and the value of n in both the log and the output is 10.

3.10.4 DO WHILE

The DO WHILE executes a group of statements while a condition is valid.

The condition is evaluated before the statements in the DO loop are executed. If the condition is not true when the condition is evaluated for the first time, the DO loop will not be executed.

Example 3.43
```
data b;
i=0;
do while(i lt 5);
i+1;
```

```
put i;
end;
run;
```

The value of `i` in the log ranges from 1 to 5. The last value of `i` in the output is 5.

TIP: Under the following conditions, you may get into an infinite loop.
1.   *By deleting the line* `i + 1;` *inside the loop body*
2.   *By deleting insert the line* `i = 0;` *inside the loop.*
In case1, by deleting the line `i + 1;`, *you are creating a permanent condition. The value of* `i` *will be fixed at zero. The same argument holds for the second case(* `i = 0`*). In the program above also notice that if the condition* `i > 5` *is changed to* `i>= 5` *the value of* `i` *in the output and in the log is 6 instead of 5. This is because the value of* `i` *is increased at the beginning of the loop and the condition is checked; the value of* `i` *is 6 so the loop stops executing. In the preceding program, if you change the value of* `i` *from 0 to 8 (a number larger than 5), the loop is never executed.*

Both DO UNTIL and DO WHILE can produce the same output given equivalent conditions.

3.11 Processing data using SAS ARRAY

If you are writing the same line of program many times, you must consider using SAS ARRAY. Look at the following programs, only one of which is using ARRAY:

Example 3.44
```
data a;
input name $ empid $ zip $ tel $;
array m(3) empid zip tel;
do i=1 to 3;
if m(i) = . then m(i) = 'Missing';
end;
drop i;
cards;
john . 303 5500999
mary 134 . 5502323
boby 156 678 .
;
run;

proc print data=a;
run;
```

Output:

```
                    The SAS System        10:06 Wednesday, March 10, 2004
                    Obs      name     empid       zip          tel
                     1       john     Missing     303        5500999
                     2       mary     134         Missing    5502323
                     3       boby     156         678        Missing
```

```
data b;
input name $ empid $ zip $ tel $;
*array m(3) empid zip tel;
if empid = . then empid ='Missing';
if zip = . then zip ='Missing';
if tel = . then tel = 'Missing';
cards;
john . 303 5500999
mary 134 . 5502323
boby 156 678 .
;
run;
```

The output of this program is exactly the same as in the previous one.

The ARRAY statement defines a set of variables. The variables in an ARRAY must all be either numeric or character.

The ARRAY statement must contain a name and a subscript.

1. The ARRAY name can be any valid SAS name, but it cannot be the name of a variable in the same DATA step. When the following program is run, an error appears in the log results indicating that the variable name month has already been defined.

```
Data abc;
Input month;
Array month[3] jan feb mar;
Run;
```

2. The subscript shows the number of elements in the array. The subscript can be an asterisk or number(s) to specify the number and arrangement of elements in the ARRAY. The subscript must be enclosed in parentheses, brackets, or braces.

```
Array color{2} gray yellow;
Array test(2,3) test1 - test6;
```

Array test(2,3) is a multidimensional array that has two rows and three columns. The SAS system assigns the data into the array by rows. The first row will be assigned values test(1,1), test(1,2), test(1,3) before the second row is assigned a value. You can have any number of dimensions in a multidimensional array.

When the asterisk [*] is used to specify the number of elements in an array, the SAS system determines the size of the array by counting the variables assigned to the array. For instance, in

```
Array rainfall[*] janf febf marf;
```
Array rainfall will have size 3.

Since the elements of an array are usually related, they are usually processed together. The data in an array can be processed with a DO loop.

Chapter summary

This chapter explained how to investigate SAS data libraries and evaluate quality of data, sort observations, modify variables attributes, and conditionally execute SAS statements. Chapter 3 also described how to use assignment statements and accumulate subtotals and totals in a DATA step. The chapter explained how to use SAS functions to manipulate character and numeric data, how to convert character data to numeric data. Processing data using DO loops and SAS array was also explained.

Two-minute drill

- Use PROC DATASETS to list, copy, remove, or delete SAS files.
- PROC DATASETS can be used also to change a variable's information such as name, format, informat, or label.
- PROC DATASETS provides all capabilities of the CONTENTS, COPY, and APPEND procedures.
- A RUN statement is not needed to execute PROC DATASETS.
- PROC CONTENTS provides information for SAS datasets or libraries.
- PROC CONTENTS gives the name of the dataset, as well as its location, when it was created, and the host by which it was created.
- PROC CONTENTS can also obtain information about variables such as name, type, format, and informat.
- PROC SORT sorts the observations in a SAS dataset by one or more variables. The result can be stored in a new dataset or can replace the original dataset.
- PROC COPY copies a SAS data library or selected members of the library.
- PROC COPY can be used to transport SAS datasets from one host to another.
- There are four different categories of formats in the SAS system: numeric, character, date, time, and user-defined formats, which are created with the FORMAT procedure.
- FORMAT procedure defines output formats for labeling values and informats for reading data.
- A word immediately followed by a period indicates a format name.
- Formats are for writing (output) variable values.
- User-defined formats convert a value to a different form for output. For example, a numeric can be converted to a character, or a character string can be converted to another character string.
- The FORMAT procedure uses *value* and *invalue* to create two user-defined formats.
- *Value* formats convert output values into a different form.
- A word immediately followed by a period indicates an informat name.
- Informats are used for reading (input) variable values.
- User defined informats convert a numeric to a character string, or a character string to a numeric value.
- User defined informats read only character data values.
- FORMAT procedure uses *value* and *invalue* to create two defined informats.
- *Value* informats read variables and transform them into other values such as character values to numeric values, or one character string to another character string.
- The *invalue* statement generates value informats.
- When FORMAT and INFORMAT are used in a DATA step to create a SAS dataset, the FORMAT and INFORMAT statements permanently associate the format or informat with a variable.
- When using FORMAT and INFORMAT in a PROC step, the FORMAT and INFORMAT statements associate the format with a variable for the duration of that step.
- PROC FREQ counts the number (frequency) of occurrences of each variable.
- PROC FREQ produces printed output by default.

- PROC FREQ can be used to analyze relationships among variables.
- To create a two-way table, state the variable names separated by an asterisk.
- The variable's type can be either numeric or character.
- PROC FREQ is distinguished for its ability to compute Chi-square tests and to compute measure of association for two-way and n-way tables.
- PROC MEANS produces statistics for numeric variables.
- PROC MEANS produces output by default.
- PROC MEANS produces statistics for the entire dataset or a subset of it.
- If no specific statistics are requested, PROC MEANS prints the name of the variable, N, MEAN, STD, MIN, and MAX.
- To get a specific statistic, mention the statistic in the PROC MEANS statement.
- Variables mentioned in the CLASS statement of PROC MEANS can be of either numeric or character type.
- You can use as many OUTPUT statements as needed with PROC MEANS.
- PROC SUMMARY produces summary statistics for numeric variables.
- PROC SUMMARY does not produce printed output by default.
- If VAR statement is omitted with PROC SUMMARY, the output will consist of a count of the observations only.
- PROC SUMMARY outputs the result of its analysis to a new SAS dataset.
- PROC SORT is controlled by the PROC SORT and BY statements.
- The BY statement is required in the SORT procedure.
- If a BY statement is not used with PROC SORT, a syntax error will be generated.
- PROC SORT sorts a dataset by one or more variables, either storing the result in a new SAS dataset or replacing the original one.
- PROC SORT rearranges data in ascending order by default.
- When using PROC SORT, the sorting order is as follows: missing, negative, zero, and then positive values.
- When using PROC SORT with character data the order is as follows: blank, lowercase letters, uppercase letters, and then digit values.
- In order to sort in descending order, use the word *descending* in the BY statement.
- Any number of variables can be specified in the BY statement.
- If an *OUT=* option appears in the sort statement, then a new dataset containing the sorted data is produced. Otherwise, the original dataset will be replaced by the sorted one.
- A compressed dataset can be sorted similar to a noncompressed dataset, but the resulting dataset will also be compressed.
- If non compressed data is to be sorted and stored in a compressed data set the option compress = yes must be explicitly stated.
- Data set options are those that appear after a SAS data set name, inside parentheses; they only apply to the data set with which they appear.
- All data set options must be followed by an equal sign.
- To use a conditional statement you must mention *where*, not *if*.
- SAS variable names can be up to 32 characters length and, must begin with a letter or an underscore followed by letters, digits, or underscore. Blanks are not allowed.
- If the type of a variable is not explicitly defined, its type is defined on initial appearance of the variable.

- If a character value is assigned to a numeric variable, SAS tries to convert it. If it can't do the conversion an error message will be sent to the log, and a missing value (a dot) will be sent to the output.
- Length of a numeric variable affects only the output, but the length of a character variable affects both input and output.
- If the length of a variable is not explicitly defined, its length is defined on initial appearance of the variable.
- INFORMAT is the instruction that SAS uses to read data values.
- FORMAT is the instruction that SAS uses to print data values.
- If you are using conditional statements in a program, use a WHERE statement to improve the efficiency of your program. The WHERE statement doesn't require the SAS system to read all observations in the input dataset.
- A WHERE statement has priority over a BY statement.
- SAS functions cannot be used in WHERE expressions.
- The IF statement selects observations from a SAS dataset or a raw dataset.
- The IF statement is executable, while the WHERE statement is not.
- An IF statement cannot be used in a PROC step.
- SELECT is an efficient alternative to an IF-THEN/ELSE statement.
- When a variable is mentioned for the first time on the left side of an assignment statement, it obtains the type of the result of the right side.
- If a variable appears for the first time on the right side of an assignment statement, the SAS system assumes its type to be numeric and its value as missing.
- A subsequent LENGTH statement can change the length of a numeric variable but not of a character variable.
- The SUM statement adds the value of a variable to an accumulator. The value of a variable is set to zero before the SAS system reads the first observation. If the first value of the variable is to differ from zero, the initial value must be included in a RETAIN statement.
- Arguments of a SAS function can be constants, names, or expressions that may include other functions.
- SAS function arguments must be preceded by the word *of* or must be separated by commas.
- SAS functions can be used in both the DATA step and in procedure programming.
- The arguments of the functions MAX, MIN, and SUM are numeric. Each of these functions must have at least two arguments.
- The function MEAN must have at least one argument.
- The function PUT can be used to write the value of a source with a specific format. The result of this function is always a character. You can use a PUT function to convert a numeric value to a character value.
- The INPUT function can be used to convert character data values to numeric ones.
- The COMPRESS function removes blanks or characters from a character expression.
- The LEFT function moves the blanks from the beginning of a value to the end of it.
- The TRIM function removes blanks at the end of an argument.
- The DATE function returns the value of today's date as the number of days from January 1, 1960.
- The DAY function returns an integer as the number of the day of the month.

- To end a DO group processing, an END statement is needed.
- DO UNTIL continues executing a group of statements until a condition is satisfied.
- DO WHILE executes a group of statements while a condition is true.
- The condition in the DO WHILE is evaluated before the statements in the DO loop are executed.
- Both DO UNTIL and DO WHILE can produce the same output given equivalent conditions.
- The variables in an ARRAY must either be all numeric or all character.
- The ARRAY statement must contain a name and at least a subscript.

Assessment exam

1. Do we need a RUN statement to execute PROC DATASETS?
2. Can we change the name of a dataset using PROC DATASETS?
3. Can we delete a dataset using PROC DATASETS?
4. Which one of the following two procedures PROC DATASETS or PROC CONTENTS can we use to find the host by which a dataset was created?.
5. Can we use PROC CONTENTS to find the time when a dataset was created?
6. Can we use PROC SORT to sort a SAS dataset by more than one variable?
7. Which procedure should we use to transport a SAS dataset from one host to another?
8. How many different categories of FORMATS are there in the SAS system?
9. Name different categories of SAS FORMATS.
10. What is the definition of a format name in the SAS system?
11. Are FORMATS intended for reading data values or writing them?
12. Does PROC FREQ produce a printed output by default?
13. Using PROC FREQ, how do you create a n-way table?
14. What is the distinguishing feature of PROC FREQ?
15. PROC MEANS produce statistics for what type of variable?
16. Does PROC MEANS produce output by default?
17. For which one of the following datasets can PROC MEANS produce statistics: a subset of a dataset, the entire dataset, or both?
18. If no statistics are requested from PROC MEANS, what does this procedure output?
19. How do you request a specific statistic with PROC MEANS?
20. When using PROC MEANS, what is the type of CLASS variable?
21. How many OUTPUT statements can you have with PROC MEANS?
22. Does PROC SUMMARY produce a printed output by default?
23. If the VAR statement is omitted in PROC SUMMARY, what is the output of PROC SUMMARY?
24. When using PROC SORT, apart from the PROC SORT statement, what is the other requirement?
25. When using PROC SORT to sort numeric values, what are the smallest and the largest values?
26. When using PROC SORT to sort observations, what is the default order?
27. When do you use the COMPRESS option?
28. Name two of the SAS variable attributes.
29. What can a name of a SAS variable begin with?
30. To what do dataset options apply?
31. Output options can appear only in __?
32. Name the conditional statements.
33. Which one is more efficient, the IF or the WHERE statement?
34. Can you use the WHERE statement with an external file containing raw data?
35. In a DATA step, if you have both the WHERE and the BY statements, which one is executed first?
36. Name two of the operators that are valid only for the WHERE expression.

37. Can you use an IF statement in a PROC step?
38. Can you use a WHERE statement to select observations from a raw dataset?
39. Name a statement which is an efficient alternative to the IF-THEN/ELSE statement.
40. Can a subsequent LENGTH statement change the length of a character variable?
41. Can the arguments of a SAS function include other functions?
42. MAX and MIN functions need at least two arguments. At least how many arguments does the MEAN function need?
43. Does the LEFT function change the length of a variable?
44. The DATE function retains the number of days from a specific date. What is that date?
45. What is the result of the DAY function?
46. If you place the SUBSTR function on the right side of an assignment, what does it return?
47. Which function would you use to convert a character value to a numeric one?
48. What do you need in order to end group processing?
49. What is (are) the necessary component(s) of an ARRAY?

Assessment exam answers

1. No.
2. Yes.
3. Yes.
4. PROC CONTENTS.
5. Yes.
6. Yes.
7. PROC COPY.
8. Four.
9. Numeric, character, date and time, user-defined.
10. A word immediately followed by a period.
11. It is intended for reading data values.
12. Yes
13. Separate variable names by asterisks in the TABLE statement.
14. By its ability to compute Chi-square tests and measures of association for two-way and n-way tables.
15. Numeric.
16. Yes.
17. For both a subset of a dataset and the entire dataset.
18. It prints the name of variables, N, MEAN, STD, MIN, MAX.
19. By mentioning it in the PROC MEANS statement.
20. Either numeric or character.
21. As many as you wish.
22. No.
23. A count of observations.
24. BY statement.
25. Smallest are missing values; largest are positive values.
26. Ascending.
27. When creating a new dataset.
28. Name, type.
29. A letter or an underscore.

30. They apply to dataset with which they appear.
31. DATA statement.
32. WHERE, IF, IF–THEN/ELSE, SELECT.
33. The WHERE statement is more efficient.
34. No.
35. The WHERE statement executes before the BY statement.
36. BETWEEN–AND and CONTAIN.
37. No.
38. No.
39. SELECT statement.
40. No.
41. Yes.
42. One.
43. No.
44. January 1, 1960.
45. Day of the month.
46. It returns a portion of an expression that is specified in the argument beginning with the position you mention.
47. The INPUT function.
48. An END statement.
49. A name and a subscript.

Practice exam

1. Which one of the following SAS procedures doesn't need a RUN statement in order to be executed?
    A. MEANS
    B. FREQ
    C. DATASETS
    D. REPORT

2. In order to delete a dataset, which one of the following statements of PROC DATASETS should be used?
    A. Eliminate
    B. Remove
    C. Change *name of data set* to
    D. Delete

3. Using PROC DATASETS, which one of the following moves a temporary dataset to a permanent library?
    A. `libname old 'c:\mydata'; proc datasets lib=work; copy out=old;`
    B. `libname old 'c:\mydata'; proc datasets lib=temp; copy out=old;`
    C. `libname old 'c:\mydata'; proc datasets lib=mydata; copy out=old;`
    D. `libname old 'c:\mydata'; proc datasets lib=SAS; copy out=old;`

4. Which of the following SAS procedures provides information about SAS datasets or libraries?
    A. DATASETS
    B. MEANS
    C. FREQ
    D. CONTENTS

5. Which one of the following procedures provides the number of occurrences of each variable?
    A. MEANS
    B. FREQ
    C. DATASETS
    D. CONTENTS

6. PROC MEANS provides statistics for
    A. Numeric variables.
    B. Character variables.
    C. Both numeric and character variables.
    D. Depending on the dataset subset, it can provide for either numeric or character variables.

7. When using PROC SORT, what is the sorting order of numeric variables?
   A. Negative, zero, positive, missing
   B. Missing, zero, negative, positive
   C. Missing, negative, zero, positive,
   D. Missing, positive, zero, negative

8. Which one of the following procedures is distinguished by its ability to provide the Chi-square test?
   A. MEANS
   B. DATASETS
   C. FREQ
   D. SORT

9. The MAX function
   A. Needs at least one argument
   B. Can't have a missing value as one of its arguments
   C. Needs at least two arguments
   D. Can use OF with all arguments as numbers.

10. The MEAN function needs at least
    A. One argument
    B. Two arguments
    C. Three arguments
    D. Four arguments

11. The result of the PUT function is
    A. Always a numeric value
    B. Always a character value
    C. Either numeric or character
    D. Conversion of a character value to a numeric one

12. The COMPRESS function
    A. Inserts characters or blanks into a character expression
    B. Removes characters or blanks from a character expression
    C. Inserts only blanks into a character expression
    D. Removes only characters from a character expression

13. The TRIM function
    A. Removes all blanks from an argument
    B. Removes blanks at the beginning of an argument
    C. Removes blanks at the end of an argument
    D. Removes blanks, which are in the middle of an argument

14. The DAY function returns the number of
    A. Days from January 1, 1960
    B. Day of the week
    C. Day of the year
    D. Day of the month

15. The SUBSTR function has
    A. Two operations
    B. One operation
    C. Three operations
    D. As many operations as it needs, depending on the string expression

16. The INDEX function returns
    A. The position of the first character of the string it is searching for
    B. The position of the last character of the string it is searching for
    C. A value of zero, if it can't find the string it is looking for
    D. A value of one, if it can't find the string it is looking for

17. What is the output of the following program?
```
libname a 'c:\mydata';
data tax7;
set a.books;
if listprice le 19.99 then do;
taxrate=.07;
else taxrate = .09;
end;
tax = listprice*taxrate;
run;
proc print data=tax7;
run;
```
    A. The tax on books with `listprice` less than 19.99 is calculated.
    B. The tax on books with `list price` less than 19.99 is calculated at the rate of 7%
        and the books with `listprice` higher than 19.99 is calculated at the rate of 9%
    C. There is no output.
    D. The taxes on all books are calculated at the rate of 7%

18. Which one of the following is not correct?
    A. `do I = 100 to 1 by 2;`
    B. `do I = 100;`
    C. `do m = 'jan','feb','mar';`
    D. `do n = 10,100, 1000`

19. How many lines of observation will the following program produce?
```
data b;
do i = 1 to 18 by -2;
y = i + 1;
```

```
output;
end;
run;
```
A. One
B. 8
C. 9
D. none

20. On execution of the following program, what are the values of i and y?
```
data b;
do i = 2 to 18 by 2;
y = i + 1;
end;
run;
```
A. $i = 20, y = 19$
B. $i = 19, y = 20$
C. $i = 18, y = 20$
D. $i = 20, y = 18$

21. When you use UNTIL and WHILE clauses in the iterative DO, which one of the following is correct?
A. The value of WHILE is evaluated after execution of each iteration of the DO loop.
B. The value of WHILE is evaluated before execution of each iteration of the DO loop.
C. The value of UNTIL is evaluated before execution of each iteration of the DO loop.
D. Both A and C.

22. After execution of the following program what are the values of i and y?
```
data c;
x = 4;
do i = 1 to 10 while(x>y);
y = i + 1;
output;
end;
run;
```
A. $i = 4, y = 5$
B. $i = 4, y = 4$
C. $i = 3, y = 4$
D. $i = 4, y = 3$

23. On execution of the following program, what are the values of i and y?
```
data c;
x = 4;
do i = 1 to 10 until(x<y);
y = i + 1;
output;
end;
run;
```

A. $i = 4, y = 5$
B. $i = 3, y = 4$
C. $i = 5, y = 5$
D. $i = 4, y = 4$

24. How many lines of output will the following program produce?
```
data a;
n=0;
do until(n>=5);
n+1;
put n;
end;
run;
```
A. 0
B. 1
C. 5
D. 6

25. DO UNTIL checks the condition
   A. At the top of the loop
   B. At the bottom of the loop
   C. Both A and B
   D. None of the above

26. Once the following program is executed, what is the value of n?
```
data a;
n=0;
do until(n>=5);
n+1;
put n;
end;
run;
```
A. 6
B. 7
C. 4
D. 5

27. After execution of the following program, what is the value of i?
```
data b;
i=0;
do while(i le 5);
i+1;
put i;
end;
run;
```

A. 6
B. 5
C. 4
D. 7

28. Consider the program in question 27. Under which of the following will you create an infinite loop?
    A. If the PUT statement is deleted
    B. If the END statement is deleted
    C. If the line `i + 1;` is deleted
    D. If the line `i = 0;` is deleted

29. An ARAY statement defines:
    A. A DO loop
    B. The beginning of a DATA step
    C. The beginning of a PROC step
    D. A set of variables

30. Variables in an ARRAY must all be of
    A. Numeric type
    B. Character type
    C. Either all numeric or all character type
    D. Date type

31. An ARARY statement must contain
    A. A DO loop
    B. A subscript, a name
    C. A name
    D. Both B and C

32. What is the result on the execution of the following program?
    ```
    data a;
    input name $;
    array name(4) week1 week2 week3 week4;
    run;
    ```
    A. An error message in the log
    B. An array with three variables
    C. An array with nine variables
    D. An array with one variable.

Practice exam answers

1. C
2. D

3. A
4. D
5. B
6. A
7. C
8. C
9. C
10. A
11. B
12. B
13. C
14. D
15. A
16. A
17. C
18. A
19. D
20. A
21. B
22. C
23. A
24. B
25. B
26. D
27. A
28. C
29. D
30. C
31. D
32. A

Problems

1. The following dataset is given. Write a program to delete the people with the same Social Security number (ss#):
    ```
    Adams 288334567 22 peachtree rd 404-352-3535
    Vavan 123987123 13 kings circle 303-454-3223
    Johns 288334567 455 dikwood rd 770-981-8989
    ```

2. Repeat problem 1, this time eliminating observations that are exactly the same. The following changes in the data set should be made:
    ```
    Johns 288334567 455 dikwood rd 770-981-8989
    Vavan 123987123 13 kings circle 303-454-3223
    Johns 288334567 455 dikwood rd 770-981-8989
    ```

3. Calculate the percentage of salary of each employee in terms of the mean salary of all employees. Use the following dataset to test your program:
    ```
    100 Bore 23000
    200 wood 59900
    300 Vohn 89500
    400 Quin 76900
    ```

4. Suppose that you have a dataset that includes Social Security numbers. These numbers are entered in two different ways, one with dashes and the other one with no dash. Write a program to place the ones with dashes in a dataset called DASH and the other one in a dataset called DIGIT:
    ```
    222-333-444
    123456789
    ```

5. Consider the following dataset. Write a program to omit all dashes and parentheses.
    ```
    (404)333-5232
    770-676-7789
    ```

6. In the given dataset employee id – empid – has a length of 6, which contains a four-digit number and two characters representing the state where the employee is stationed. Write a program to place employees who are working in the state of Georgia in a separate dataset called GA:
    ```
    jordan 3214GA sales
    hudkin 8912CA acctpay
    whites 5687GA finance
    ```

7. You have a data set named BONUS that contains the bonuses that employees have received for four different seasons (one per season). The dataset has three variables, empid, bonus1, bonus2, bonus3, bonus4, as follows:
    ```
    101 2500 1900 1400 2600
    102 850 1120 980 1300
    103 750 680 980 990
    ```
    You are asked to create a new dataset with four observations for each employee (showing bonuses of each employee for each season on a separate line).

8. Modify your program in problem 7 to change the name of seasons from 1, 2, 3, 4 to winter, spring, summer, and fall, respectively.

9. Suppose that you have the dataset BOOKS (you have seen it before in this book) that has information about different books and their publishers. You are asked to write a program to count only the frequencies of each publisher in this dataset.

Problem solutions

```
1. data aa;
   input name $ ssnum 9. address $ 17. telnum $ 12.;
   cards;
   Adams 288334567 22 peachtree rd 404-352-3535
   Vavan 123987123 13 kings circle 303-454-3223
   Johns 288334567 45 dikwood rd   770-981-8989
   ;
   run;
   proc sort data=aa nodupkey out=bb;
   by descending ssnum;
   run;
   proc print data=bb;
   run;
```
Output:

```
The SAS System        08:55 Sunday, February 20, 2005
             Obs    name     ssnum        address         telnum
              1     Adams   288334567   22 peachtree rd   404-352-3535
              2     Vavan   123987123   13 kings circle   303-454-3223
```

```
2. data cc;
   input name $ ssnum 9. address $ 17. telnum $ 12.;
   cards;
   Johns 288334567 455 dikwood rd 770-981-8989
   Vavan 123987123 13 kings circle 303-454-3223
   Johns 288334567 455 dikwood rd 770-981-8989
   ;
   run;
   proc sort data=aa nodupkey out=dd;
   by descending ssnum;
   run;
   proc print data=dd;
   run;
```

Output:

```
The SAS System        08:55 Sunday, February 20, 2005    9
     Obs    name      ssnum          address          telnum
     1      Johns     288334567      455 dikwood rd 7  70-981-8989
     2      Vavan     123987123      13 kings circle   303-454-3223
```

3.
```
data employ;
input id name $ salary;
cards;
100 Bore 23000
200 wood 59900
300 Vohn 89500
400 Quin 76900
;
run;
proc means data=employ mean;
var salary;
output out=newemp mean=meansal;
run;
data percsal;
set employ;
if _n_=1 then set newemp;
perc_sal=100*salary/meansal;
run;
proc print data=percsal(keep=name salary meansal perc_sal);
run;
```

Output:

```
The SAS System        08:55 Sunday, February 20, 2005

          Obs    name    salary    meansal    perc_sal
          1      Bore     23000     62325      36.903
          2      wood     59900     62325      96.109
          3      Vohn     89500     62325     143.602
          4      Quin     76900     62325     123.385
```

4.
```
data dash digit;
input ssnum $ 11.;
if index(ssnum,'-') eq 4 or index(ssnum,'-') eq 8 then
output dash;
else output digit;
cards;
```

```
222-333-444
123456789
;
run;
proc print data=dash;
title 'DATA SET DASH';
run;
proc print data=digit;
title 'DATA SET DIGIT';
run;
```

Output:

```
DATA SET DASH        15:19 Monday, February 21, 2005
                                  Obs        ssnum
                                   1      222-333-444

DATA SET DIGIT       15:19 Monday, February 21, 2005
                                  Obs        ssnum
                                   1       123456789
```

5.
```
data ab;
input telnum $ 11.;
telnumber=compress(telnum,'()-');
cards;
(404)333-5232
770-676-7789
;
run;
proc print data=ab;
run;
```

Output:

```
The SAS System       15:19 Monday, February 21, 2005
                     Obs      telnum        telnumber
                      1    (404)333-52      40433352
                      2    770-676-778      770676778
```

6.
```
data a GA;
input name $ empid $ dept $;
if substr(empid,5,2)='GA' then output GA;
else output a;
cards;
jordan 3214GA sales
hudkin 8912CA acctpay
```

```
whites 5687GA finance
;
run;
proc print data=GA;
run;
```

Output:

```
                 The SAS System     08:53 Tuesday, February 22, 2005
                            Obs      name      empid      dept
                             1       jordan    3214GA     sales
                             2       whites    5687GA     finance
```

7.
```
data bonus;
input empid bonus1 bonus2 bonus3 bonus4;
cards;
101 2500 1900 1400 2600
102 850 1120 980 1300
103 750 680 980 990
;
run;
data seas_bon;
set bonus;
array yy(4) bonus1-bonus4;
do season = 1 to 4;
seabonu = yy(season);
output;
end;
run;
proc print data=seas_bon(drop=bonus1 bonus2 bonus3 bonus4);
run;
```

Output:

```
         The SAS System     07:48 Thursday, February 24, 2005
                    Obs      empid     season     seabonu
                      1       101         1         2500
                      2       101         2         1900
                      3       101         3         1400
                      4       101         4         2600
                      5       102         1          850
                      6       102         2         1120
                      7       102         3          980
                      8       102         4         1300
                      9       103         1          750
                     10       103         2          680
                     11       103         3          980
                     12       103         4          990
```

```
8. data snambo;
   set bonus;
   array nambno(4) bonus1-bonus4;
   do i=1 to 4;
   if i=1 then season='winter';
   else if i=2 then season='spring';
   else if i=3 then season='summer';
   else if i=4 then season='fall';
   seabonu = nambno(i);
   output;
   end;
   run;
   proc print data=snambo(keep=empid season seabonu);
   run;
```

Output:

```
The SAS System      07:48 Thursday, February 24, 2005
                    Obs    empid    season    seabonu
                     1      101     winter     2500
                     2      101     spring     1900
                     3      101     summer     1400
                     4      101     fall       2600
                     5      102     winter      850
                     6      102     spring     1120
                     7      102     summer      980
                     8      102     fall       1300
                     9      103     winter      750
                    10      103     spring      680
                    11      103     summer      980
                    12      103     fall        990
```

```
9. libname a 'c:\mydata';
   proc freq data=a.books;
   tables publisher/nocum nopercent;
   run;
```

Output:

```
The SAS System      07:48 Thursday, February 24, 2005
                                   The FREQ Procedure
                           publisher     Frequency

                           barnes           1
                           barns            2
                           borders          2
                           mcgraw           1
                           oxford           3
```

4   Generating Reports

Certification objectives

In this chapter you will learn what you need to pass this section of the exam:

- **Generating list reports using the PRINT and REPORT procedures**
- **Generating summary reports and frequency tables using Base SAS procedures**
- **Enhancing reports through the use of titles, footnotes, labels, SAS formats, user-defined formats, and the SAS system reporting options**
- **Generating HTML reports using ODS statements**

In this chapter you will learn how to generate list reports using the PRINT and REPORT procedures. You will learn how to enhance reports through the use of titles, footnotes, labels, SAS formats, user-defined formats, and SAS system reporting options. You will also generate HTML reports using ODS statements.

At the end of this chapter you can review its material by reading the two-minute drill, then taking the practice test to see how well you understand and retain the material. Answers to these questions are provided at the end of the test. A set of problems with solutions is also provided for further practice.

4.1 Generating list reports using the PRINT and REPORT procedures

4.1.1 PRINT procedure

The PRINT procedure can be used to print the values of all or some of the variables. A report can be customized in many different ways, using the options of the PRINT procedure. The totals and subtotals of numeric variables in the dataset can be calculated using the PRINT procedure. In the following example the PRINT procedure will print the content of dataset books.

Example 4.1
```
libname a 'c:\mydata';
proc print data=a.books;
run;
```

If the option data= is not used, the PRINT procedure will print the most recently created dataset.

We can use the following options with PRINT procedure:
VAR
TITLE
LABEL
BY
SUM

VAR

Use the `var` option to print the values of only those variables needed in the output:

Example 4.2

```
libname a 'c:\mydata';
proc print data=a.books;
var title publisher listprice;
run;
```

Output:

```
The SAS System        10:25 Tuesday, March 23, 2004    1
                  Obs    title      publisher    listprice
                   1     algebra    barnes         $10.55
                   2     music      borders        $11.95
                   3     pastry     oxford         $15.99
                   4     guitar     borders        $21.99
                   5     maths      barns           $8.00
                   6     bagels     oxford         $19.50
                   7     manageme   oxford         $28.50
                   8     fortran    mcgraw         $40.00
                   9     44.98      barns          $45.99
                  10     Maths      Mcgraw         $74.99
                  11     Algebra    Barnes         $88.95
                  12     Food       Barnes         $10.99
```

TITLE

A title can be added to the output of a program by using the TITLE statement. The following example shows the syntax of the TITLE statement.

Example 4.3

```
libname a 'c:\mydata';
proc print data=a.books;
var title publisher listprice;
format listprice dollar7.2;
sum listprice;
title 'THIS IS A BRIEF REPORT';
run;
```

Output:

```
THIS IS A BRIEF REPORT    10:46 Tuesday, March 23, 2004
                          Obs     title      publisher      listprice
                           1      algebra    barnes          $10.55
                           2      music      borders         $11.95
                           3      pastry     oxford          $15.99
                           4      guitar     borders         $21.99
                           5      maths      barns           $8.00
                           6      bagels     oxford          $19.50
                           7      manageme   oxford          $28.50
                           8      fortran    mcgraw          $40.00
                           9      44.98      barns           $45.99
                          10      Maths      Mcgraw          $74.99
                          11      Algebra    Barnes          $88.95
                          12      Food       Barnes          $10.99
                                                          ==========
                                                            $377.40
```

LABEL

To make headings more explicit, use the `label` option , by mentioning it in the first line of PROC PRINT, otherwise the LABEL statement will be ignored by SAS system.

Example 4.4
```
libname a 'c:\mydata';
proc print data=a.books label;
label publisher='ACTUAL PUBLISHER';
run;
```

To conserve space in the output, the label can be split by including `split='*'` in the first line of PROC PRINT, and an asterisk in the `label` option.

Example 4.5
```
libname a 'c:\mydata';
proc print data=a.books split='*';
var cost publisher;
label publisher='ACTUAL*PUBLISHER';
run;
```

Output:

```
SAS System               17:10 Sunday, April 4, 2004
                                                ACTUAL
                         Obs      cost        PUBLISHER
                          1      $10.25        barns
                          2      $12.95        barnes
                          3      $15.99        borders
                          4      $18.95        oxford
                          5      $19.95        borders
                          6      $24.99        oxford
                          7      $31.95        oxford
                          8      $46.99        mcgraw
                          9      $51.50        barns
```

Remember that you split the label not the title. The LABEL option is discussed further in Section 4.3.

BY

When you use a BY statement, the PRINT procedure prints a separate analysis for each BY group. Before using BY, you must sort the data by the variable mentioned in the BY statement.

Example 4.6

```
data b;
input emp $ salary bonus;
cards;
ali 34000 2300
ali 50000 99
jil 55000 4200
jil 60000 88
;
run;
proc print data=b;
by salary;
run;
```

Output:

```
The SAS System            17:10 Sunday, April 4, 2004   8
------------------------------------------- salary=34000 --------------
---
                                    Obs      emp      bonus
                                     1       ali      2300
------------------------------------------- salary=50000 --------------
---
                                    Obs      emp      bonus
                                     2       ali       99
------------------------------------------- salary=55000 --------------
---
                                    Obs      emp      bonus
                                     3       jil      4200
------------------------------------------- salary=60000 --------------
---
                                    Obs      emp      bonus
                                     4       jil       88
```

SUM

The SUM option is used to find the total value of the variables that you included in the SUM statement.

Example 4.7

```
data b;
input emp $ salary bonus;
cards;
ali 34000 2300
```

```
ali 50000 99
jil 55000 4200
jil 60000 88
;
run;
proc print data=b;
sum salary;
run;
```

Output:

```
The SAS System                    17:10 Sunday, April 4, 2004
                        Obs    emp    salary    bonus
                         1     ali    34000     2300
                         2     ali    50000       99
                         3     jil    55000     4200
                         4     jil    60000       88
                                      ======
                                      199000
```

SUM and BY can be used together.

Example 4.8
```
data b;
input emp $ salary bonus;
cards;
ali 34000 2300
ali 10000 99
jil 55000 4200
jil 20000 88
;
run;
proc print data=b;
sum salary bonus;
by emp;
run;
```

Output:

```
The SAS System            17:10 Sunday, April 4, 2004
------------------------------------------ emp=ali ------------------
                        Obs    salary    bonus
                         1     34000     2300
                         2     10000       99
                        ---    ------    -----
                        emp    44000     2399
------------------------------------------ emp=jil ------------------
                        Obs    salary    bonus
                         3     55000     4200
                         4     20000       88
                        ---    ------    -----
                        emp    75000     4288
                               ======    =====
                               119000    6687
```

4.1.2 REPORT procedure

The REPORT procedure is a very powerful report-generating tool; it can produce both detailed reports and summary reports, and combines the features of the three procedures PRINT, MEANS, and TABULATES. A report can be customized by using the many options of this procedure.

To create a list report, use the PROC REPORT statement, which invokes the report procedure. Secify the input data on the PROC REPORT statement DATA = option. If the output report is to go to a specific dataset, mention the dataset name on the first line in the OUT = option.

A simple PROC REPORT program is as follows:

```
Proc report data=a ;
Run;
```

PROC REPORT produces an output by default.

OPTIONS of PROC REPORT
Many options can be used with the PROC REPORT statement, including the following:
NOWD
COLUMN
WHERE
DEFINE
ORDER
ANALYSIS
SUMMARIZE
COMPUTE
BY

1. NOWD. Using NOWD allows the SAS system to execute the subsequent SAS statements.

Example 4.9
```
libname a 'c:\mydata';
proc report data=a.books nowd;
run;
```

TIP: Notice the NOWD at the end of the first line. If NOWD is unspecified in the report procedure statement, the SAS statements subsequent to PROC REPORT will result in the following error message: "Note: PROC REPORT is currently executing. All subsequently submitted statements will not begin executing until its completion."

Output:

```
The SAS System          15:05 Monday, November 10, 2003

cost      datesold    listprice    author      publisher    section    title
$12.95    01/01/98    $10.55       mohamad     barnes       science    algebra
$15.99    01/02/98    $11.95       davood      borders      art        music
$18.95    08/03/01    $15.99       barbara     oxford       cooking    pastry
$19.95    04/04/98    $21.99       daryoosh    borders      art        guitar
$10.25    06/06/99    $8.00        parviz      barns        science    maths
$24.99    09/08/99    $19.50       hacib       oxford       cooking    bagels
$31.95    10/10/98    $28.50       mamal       oxford       art        manageme
$46.99    11/11/01    $40.00       reza        mcgraw       science    fortran
$65.99    03/08/02    $74.99       davood      Mcgraw       science    Maths
$99.99    12/12/02    $88.95       davood      Barnes       science    Algebra
$12.95    06/09/02    $10.99       parviz      Barnes       cooking    Food
```

2. COLUMN. This option specifies the columns that will appear in the output.

Example 4.10
```
libname a 'c:\mydata';
proc report data=a.books nowd;
column author cost;
run;
```

Output :

```
The SAS System          15:05 Monday, November 10, 2003
                                        author       cost
                                        mohamad      $12.95
                                        davood       $15.99
                                        barbara      $18.95
                                        daryoosh     $19.95
                                        parviz       $10.25
                                        hacib        $24.99
                                        mamal        $31.95
                                        reza         $46.99
                                        diba         $51.50
                                        davood       $65.99
                                        davood       $99.99
                                        parviz       $12.95
```

3. WHERE. The WHERE statement selects the observations that satisfy the stated criteria.

Example 4.11
```
libname a 'c:\mydata';
```

```
proc report data=a.books nowd;
where cost lt 19.99;
run;
```

Output:

```
The SAS System          11:11 Sunday, November 16, 2003

cost     datesold    listprice   author    publisher   section   title
$10.25   06/06/98    $8.00       parviz    barns       science   maths
$12.95   01/01/98    $10.55      mohamad   barnes      science   algebra
$15.99   01/02/98    $11.95      davood    borders     art       music
$18.95   08/03/98    $15.99      barbara   oxford      cooking   pastery
$19.95   04/04/98    $21.99      daryoosh  borders     art       guitar
```

4. DEFINE. This option describes how to use and display a report item.

5. ORDER. You can change the default order by using ORDER = and DESCENDING in the DEFINE statement. By default, PROC REPORT arranges rows in ascending order.

5. ANALYSIS. This option uses the analysis variable to analyze data. The analysis variable is a numeric variable that is used to calculate statistics for a group of observations.

6. SUMMARIZE. This option writes the value of the analysis variable in the summary line.

In the following example, note the appearance of the options OL and SKIP. The OL option creates a horizontal line before each line of sum. The option SKIP skips a line after each block of calculation.

Example 4.12
```
data a;
input name $ salary;
cards;
ab 12000
bc 25000
cd 88000
ab 100000
bc 200000
cd 300000
;
proc report data=a nowd;
define name  / order;
define salary / analysis sum;
break after name / ol summarize skip;
```

```
run;
```

```
The SAS System        15:05 Monday, November 10, 2003
                                        name      salary
                                        ab         12000
                                                  100000

                                        ab        112000
                                        bc         25000
                                                  200000

                                        bc        225000
                                        cd         88000
                                                  300000

                                        cd        388000
```

8. COMPUTE. This option starts a computation block that produces a customized summary at the end of the report.

Example 4.13
```
proc report data=a nowd;
define name  / order;
define salary / analysis sum;
break after name / ol summarize skip;
compute after;
line 'Total of salary are: ' salary.sum;
endcomp;
run;
```

Output:

```
The SAS System        07:41 Tuesday, November 11, 2003  15
                                        name      salary
                                        ab         12000
                                                  100000

                                        ab        112000
                                        bc         25000
                                                  200000

                                        bc        225000
                                        cd         88000
                                                  300000

                                        cd        388000
                            Total of salary is: 725000
```

Or simply use the following:

Example 4.14
```
proc report data=a;
compute after ;
line salary.sum;
endcomp;
run;
```

Output:

```
The SAS System          11:11 Sunday, November 16, 2003
                                         name          salary
                                         ab             12000
                                         bc             25000
                                         cd             88000
                                         ab            100000
                                         bc            200000
                                         cd            300000
                                                       725000
```

9. BY. The BY statement creates a separate report on a separate page for each BY group. When using the BY statement, the OUT = option can not be used. If the BY statement is used the NOWD option must also be used in the PROC REPORT statement. The following example illustrates what happens if OUT is used with BY group:

Example 4.15
```
libname a 'c:\mydata';
proc report data=a.books out=abc nowd;
by cost;
run;
```

Log:

```
ERROR: Output data set cannot be created for BY groups.
NOTE: The SAS System stopped processing this step because of
errors.
NOTE: PROCEDURE REPORT used:
      real time           0.83 seconds
      cpu time            0.36 seconds
```

PROC REPORT requires at least one variable to form a BY group. If the observations are not sorted by the variable(s) mentioned, the NOTSORTED option must be used in the BY statement.

Example 4.16

```
data a;
input name $ salary;
cards;
ab 12000
bc 25000
cd 88000
ab 100000
bc 200000
cd 300000
;
proc report data=a nowd;
by name notsorted;
run;
```

Output:

The output is simply a one-line report with each name on a separate page. Observations with duplicates will be duplicated on separate pages.

4.2 Generating summary reports and frequency tables using Base SAS procedures

The SAS system provides different procedures to analyze data and prepare summary reports. Some of these procedures are
FREQ
MEANS
SUMMARY
TABULATES

All these procedures compute descriptive statistics and display them in tabular format. Simple or customized tables can be created using any of these procedures. The first three procedures are explained in detail in Section 3.2 of this book. In this section, we will discuss PROC TABULATE, which is the most powerful of all these procedure; it can provide all necessary statistics in a very concise table.

4.2.1 PROC TABULATE

You can use PROC TABULATE to do any or all of the following:
1. Produce one dimensional tabular reports
2. Produce two dimensional tabular reports
3. Produce three dimensional reports
4. Control the appearance of reports with the aid of options and operators of this procedure.

One-dimensional report

To create a one dimensional report, at least one TABLE statement is needed. Depending on the variable to appear in the report, a CLASS statement, a VAR statement, or both will be needed.

One, two, or three variable(s) in the TABLE statement will result in a one-, two-, or three-dimensional(1D, 2D, or 3D) table (report), respectively.

The variable mentioned in the VAR statement is called the *analysis variable,* and its type is *numeric.* If a character variable is used in a VAR statement, an error message is produced in the LOG with no output.

Variables appearing in the TABLE statement must be mentioned either in the VAR or the CLASS statement, but **not both.**

TIP: If a variable is mentioned in both the VAR and CLASS statements, the result is an error message with no output.

Variables appearing in the CLASS statement can be of either *character* or *numeric* type. If a variable is named in the CLASS statement, then the default statistic is N (the number of observations in each category of the variable). If a variable appears in the VAR statement, then the default statistic is SUM.

We will consider a simple 1D PROC TABULATE program and its concise report.

Example 4.17
```
libname a'c:\mydata';
proc tabulate data=a.books;
var cost listprice;
class author title;
table author*title;
run;
```

Output:

The SAS System	17:08 Wednesday, April 21, 2004

author								
barbara	**daryoosh**	**davood**	**diba**	**hacib**	**mamal**	**mohamad**	**parviz**	**reza**
title	title	title	title	title	title	title	title	title
cooking	art	art	art	cooking	art	science	science	science
N	**N**	**N**	**N**	**N**	**N**	**N**	**N**	**N**
1	1	1	1	1	1	1	1	1

TIP: If a statistic other than N is requested from the variable in the CLASS statement, an error message will be generated with no output. Consider the example below:

Example 4.18
```
libname a 'c:\mydata';
proc tabulate data=a.books;
class cost;
table cost*mean;
run;
```

```
Log:
Physical Name: c:\mydata
11    proc tabulate data=a.books;
12    class cost;
13    table cost*mean;
14    run;
ERROR: Statistic other than N was requested without analysis variable in the
following nesting : ost * Mean.
NOTE: The SAS System stopped processing this step because of errors.
NOTE: PROCEDURE TABULATE used:
      real time              0.00 seconds
```

To add a statistic to a table, add an asterisk (*) to the name of the variable in the TABLE statement. For example, to sum the *cost* variable use the following line of code: *table cost*sum;* .

TIP: A space is the concatenating operator in PROC TABULATE.

To obtain two statistics from a variable, use this line of code:

```
table cost*n    cost*sum;
```

The line (table cost*n*sum;) will result in an error message with no output.

Tips:
1. If a variable in a TABLE statement is mentioned without naming it in the CLASS or the VAR statement, the following error will be generated: "Type of name (cost) is unknown."

2. If a variable is named in the CLASS or the VAR statement and is not used in the TABLE statement, the SAS system ignores it.

When asterisks are used to connect an analysis variable and a class variable, the order of the items does not matter; `cost*author*mean` is equivalent to `author*cost*mean`. The order of the column headings will be swapped, but the same values are produced.

Example 4.19
```
data b;
```

```
input income education $ tax;
cards;
32000 bsc 3200
42500 msc 4100
51000 mba 5500
29000 bsc 2900
64000 msc 4200
59000 mba 5650
;

proc tabulate data=b;
var income tax;
class education;
table income*education*mean;
run;
```

Output:

The SAS System   16:58 Wednesday, April 28, 2004

income		
education		
bsc	mba	msc
Mean	Mean	Mean
30500.00	55000.00	53250.00

```
proc tabulate data=b;
var income ;
class education;
table education*income*mean;
run;
```

Output:

The SAS System   16:58 Wednesday, April 28, 2004

education		
bsc	mba	msc
income	income	income
Mean	Mean	Mean
30500.00	55000.00	53250.00

Notice the difference between the two outputs. The values are the same, but the order in which they are represented is different.

Two dimensional report

In a one-dimensional table there is one row and multiple columns. In two dimensions we take advantage of multiple rows. In this way we can fit more information on a page, the tables look better, and the format is more efficient.

We can create the second dimension by adding a comma in the TABLE statement as follows: *table education , income;*.

Example 4.20

```
proc tabulate data=b;
var income tax;
class education;
table education,income*mean;
run;
```

Output:

SAS System   09:50 Monday, May 3, 2004

	income
	Mean
education	
bsc	30500.00
mba	55000.00
msc	53250.00

Notice that the variable that appears on the left side of the comma in the `table` statement creates the row, while the one on the right makes the columns. Let's add one more analysis variable:

```
proc tabulate data=b;
var income tax;
class education;
table education,income*mean tax*mean;
run;
```

Output:

```
The SAS System              09:50 Monday, May 3, 2004     3
```

	income	tax
	Mean	**Mean**
education		
bsc	30500.00	3050.00
mba	55000.00	5575.00
msc	53250.00	4150.00

TIP: Cross-tabulation of analysis variables is not allowed. In other words, one analysis variable cannot appear in a row and another analysis variable in a column of the table statement.

If a program is run with cross-tabulation of analysis variables, an error message will be generated in the log with no output. Pay attention to the following program and the log message.

Example 4.21

```
proc tabulate data=b;
var income tax;
class education;
table tax,income;
run;
```

Log:

```
115   proc tabulate data=b;
116   var income tax;
117   class education;
118   table tax,income;
119   run;
ERROR: There are multiple analysis variables associated with a single table
cell in the following
         nesting : tax * income.
NOTE: The SAS System stopped processing this step because of errors.
NOTE: PROCEDURE TABULATE used:
      real time              0.00 seconds
```

Tips

1. In a two-dimensional table, at least one variable must be in the CLASS statement.

2. Statistics ca not be requested in both a row and a column of the TABLE statement.

Example 4.22

```
proc tabulate data=b;
var income tax;
class education;
table education*n,income*n;
run;
```

Log:

```
132   proc tabulate data=b;
133   var income tax;
134   class education;
135   table education*n,income*n;
136   run;
ERROR: There are multiple statistics associated with a single table cell in the
following nesting
        : education * N * income * N.
NOTE: The SAS System stopped processing this step because of errors.
```

```
NOTE: PROCEDURE TABULATE used:
      real time              0.05 seconds
```

The statement table education, `income*mean tax*mean;` can be rewritten as table education, (income tax)*mean;. The result will be the same.

Example 4.23
```
proc tabulate data=b;
var income tax;
class education;
table education,income*mean tax*mean;
run;
```

OR:

```
proc tabulate data=b;
var income tax;
class education;
table education,(income tax)*mean;
run;
```

They both produce the following output:

Output:

```
The SAS System              09:50 Monday, May 3, 2004
```

	income	tax
	Mean	**Mean**
education		
bsc	30500.00	3050.00
mba	55000.00	5575.00
msc	53250.00	4150.00

To add another variable to the CLASS statement; consider the following example.

Example 4.24
```
data b;
input income education $ tax gender $;
```

```
cards;
32000 bsc 3200 f
42500 msc 4100 m
51000 mba 5500 m
29000 bsc 2900 f
64000 msc 4200 m
59000 mba 5650 f
;
run;
proc tabulate data=b;
var income tax;
class education gender;
table education gender,income*mean;
run;
```

Output:

The SAS System   09:50 Monday, May 3, 2004

	income
	Mean
education	
bsc	30500.00
mba	55000.00
msc	53250.00
gender	
f	40000.00
m	52500.00

To get the row total, add ALL to the end of the column part of the TABLE statement. To get the column total, add ALL to the end of the row part of the TABLE statement.

By default, ALL is a classification variable, so there is no need to add it to the CLASS statement.

Example 4.25
```
proc tabulate data=b;
var income tax;
class education gender;
table education gender,income*mean all;
run;
```

Output:

```
The SAS System              09:50 Monday, May 3, 2004    9
```

	income	All
	Mean	N
education		
bsc	30500.00	2
mba	55000.00	2
msc	53250.00	2
gender		
f	40000.00	3
m	52500.00	3

Adding the columns; we obtain

```
proc tabulate data=b;
var income tax;
class education gender;
table education gender all,income;
run;
```

Output:

	income
	Sum
education	
bsc	61000.00
mba	110000.00
msc	106500.00
gender	
f	120000.00
m	157500.00
All	277500.00

The next example shows how to obtain subtotals for each gender in the report. Note that the word ALL goes inside the parentheses with the variable to be summed (in this case, gender).

Example 4.26
```
proc tabulate data=b;
var income tax;
class education gender;
table education*(gender all),income*mean;
run;
```

Output:

```
The SAS System          17:06 Monday, May 3, 2004    3
```

		income
		Mean
education	gender	
bsc	f	30500.00
	All	30500.00
mba	gender	
	f	59000.00
	m	51000.00
	All	55000.00
msc	gender	
	m	53250.00
	All	53250.00

Three-dimensional report

You may ask yourself "How can I create a three dimensional report on a two -dimensional paper?" Very simply, a 3D report is basically a 2D report that is extended over a few pages. In fact, the third dimension is a page.

To create a 3D table, two commas are needed in the TABLE statement:

```
table education ,gender, income ;
```

The following example provides a 3D report, consisting of a page for female and another page for male.

Example 4.27
```
proc tabulate data=b;
var income tax;
class education gender;
table gender,education,income*mean;
run;
```

Output:

The SAS System   17:06 Monday, May 3, 2004

gender f

	income
	Mean
education	
bsc	30500.00
mba	59000.00

The SAS System   17:06 Monday, May 3, 2004   11

gender m

	income
	Mean
education	
mba	51000.00
msc	53250.00

To put more tables in one page or to fit one table to a page, include the following:

```
Table education,income,gender/condense;
```

The following example, if run without the CONDENSE option, will produce one page of output for each author. The CONDENSE option tells the PROC TABULATE to fit more than one table in each page.

Example 4.28
```
libname a 'c:\mydata';
proc tabulate data=a.books;
var cost;
class author listprice ;
table author,cost,listprice/condense;
run;
```

Output:

The SAS System   11:03 Tuesday, May 4, 2004

author barbara

		listprice
		15.99
cost	**Sum**	18.95

author daryoosh

		listprice
		21.99
cost	**Sum**	19.95

author davood

	listprice
	11.95
cost	Sum	15.99

author diba

	listprice
	45.99
cost	Sum	51.50

author hacib

	listprice
	19.5
cost	Sum	24.99

author mamal

	listprice
	28.5
cost	Sum	31.95

author mohamad

		listprice
		10.55
cost	**Sum**	12.95

author parviz

		listprice
		8
cost	**Sum**	10.25

author reza

		listprice
		40
cost	**Sum**	46.99

Controling the appearance of reports with the aid of options and operators

Three different options can be used with PROC TABULATE to control the appearance of your report:
1. Options used with the PROC TABULATE statement
2. Options included in the TABLE statement
3. System options that affect the PROC TABULATE output.

1. PROC TABULATE options. As you probably know, these options appear on the line of the procedure statement. For PROC TABULATE these options include the following:
   a. DATA = name of the data set

b. DEPTH—Specifies the maximum number of elements in the coss-tabultaion.

c. FORMAT—Provides the format for numbers appearing in each cell of your report. The default is BEST12.2 which controls the size of the cell.

Example 4.29

```
libname a 'c:\mydata';
proc tabulate data=a.books format=dollar6.2;
var cost;
class author;
table author,cost;
run;
```

Output:

```
The SAS System                 11:17 Wednesday, May 5, 2004
```

	cost
	Sum
author	
barbara	$18.95
daryoosh	$19.95
davood	$15.99
diba	$51.50
hacib	$24.99
mamal	$31.95
mohamad	$12.95
parviz	$10.25
reza	$46.99

If a different format for a variable is preferred, for example, `tax`, use a line such as `Table tax*f=8.2;`

d. MISSING. This option tells the procedure to treat missing values as a valid value of the CLASS variable.

2. TABLE options

a. BOX = 'string'. BOX is the box appearing on the upper left corner of the table. The title of the report or name of a variable is usually appears here.

Example 4.30

```
libname a 'c:\mydata';
proc tabulate data=a.books format=dollar6.2;
var cost;
class author;
table author,cost/box='SALE OF BOOKS';
run;
```

Output:

The SAS System   11:17 Wednesday, May 5, 2004   4

SALE OF BOOKS	cost Sum
author	
barbara	$18.95
daryoosh	$19.95
davood	$15.99
diba	$51.50
hacib	$24.99
mamal	$31.95
mohamad	$12.95
parviz	$10.25
reza	$46.99

b. CONDENSE. This option fits more information on a page. For more information on this option see previous section.

c. MISSTEXT. This option outputs text in place of a 'dot' for missing values instead of

the default value (a dot '.')

3. System options:

a. LINSIZE = number

b. PAGESIZE = number. Specifies how much text should be put in each page of the report.

c. FORMCHAR = 'string'. This is a PROC TABULATE option and specifies which symbols can be used for the borders of the table. The following code will put plus signs + on the border of the table.

Example 4.31
```
libname a 'c:\mydata';
proc tabulate data=a.books formchar='+';
var listprice;
class author;
table author;
run;
```

Output:

```
 The SAS System              11:17 Wednesday, May 5, 2004    2


                                +          author         +
                                +   parviz    +    reza    +
                                +     N       +     N      +
                                +       1.00+        1.00+
```

d. CENTER | NOCENTER.
This option enables you to place your table on the page anywhere you desire. The following code aligns the table on the left side of the page:

```
Option nocenter;
Proc tabulate data=a;
```

SAS statements

4.3 Enhancing reports using titles, footnotes, labels, SAS formats, user–defined formats, and SAS system reporting options

4.3.1 TITLE

Title<n><text>;

TITLE statements specify titles for SAS output. Each TITLE statement specifies one title line. The title number n, varies from 1 to 10. The following are some valid TITLE statements:

```
Title 'TOTAL SALE';
Title1 'TOTAL TAX PAID';
Title2 'END OF THE REPORT';
```

A TITLE becomes effective when the step gets executed. After a TITLE takes effect, it is used for all subsequent output until it is canceled or replaced, by another TITLE statement. To cancel a TITLE statement, simply insert a new TITLE statement without an argument. All TITLE statements with larger *n* are then canceled. Up to 10 TITLE statements are permitted.

TIP: If there are two TITLE statements with the same argument n the SAS system will print the second one. For example, if the following statements appear sequentially, This is this year's tax will be printed:

```
title1 "This is last year's tax";
title1 "This is this year's tax";
```
The reason for the double quotation marks about the title is the prsscessive construction apostrophe between the year and s.

4.3.2 FOOTNOTE

Footnote<n><text>;

FOOTNOTE statements print text at the bottom of the output from a procedure and become effective when the step gets executed. The footnote number, n, ranges from 1 to 10. If *n* is omitted, SAS assigns a default value of one. The footnote with lowest n will appear on the highest line. These are some valid footnote statements:

```
Footnote 'This is title one';
Footnote1 'This another title';
```

TIP: If there are two FOOTNOTE statements with the same argument n, SAS will print the second one, similar to TITLE statement. For example

Footnote3 "This is last year's income";

Footnote3 "This is this year's income";
will cause the SAS system to print.
This is this year's income. The reason for the double quotation marks about footnote is the apostrophe between year and *s.*

4.3.3 LABEL

A *label* is a string of up to 256 characters that can be used in certain procedures in place of a variable name. LABLE is valid in a SAS OPTIONS statement.
`label=` option also be used on the input and output datasets. To remove a label from a dataset, insert a label with a blank in the enclosing quotation marks:
```
Label tax = 'Income tax';
Label income = "This year's income";
```
Here, `tax` and `income` are the names of two variables in a dataset.
You can read more about LABEL in Section 4.1.1 of this chapter.

4.3.4 FORMAT

FORMAT is a set of instructions that tells SAS how to *write* an output data value.
This is the syntax of a SAS FORMAT statement:

```
<$>format<w>.<d>
```

To specify that a value is of character type, you must use a dollar($) sign; otherwise SAS will assume that the value is a numeric one.
In the syntax displayed above, `W` specifies the total number of columns to be assigned for the data value including columns for minus signs, commas, or dollar signs if applicable, and d indicates the number of columns to be assigned for decimal places in the data value. Some examples are
```
format name $ 10. ;
format salary 12.2;
format words20.;
```
They all write the number 123 as *one hundred twenty-three.*

A FORMAT must always have a period (.). In another words, a FORMAT is a name that contains a period. For example, `dollar6.2` represents a format that has six columns in total, and two of these columns are considered for decimal places in the data value. The number 6 in this case includes a minus sign if the value is negative, or a comma or a dollar sign if applicable.
Remember that when using a FORMAT statement the `format` is associated with the variable *permanently.*

User-defined FORMAT
SAS programmers can write their own formats by using PROC FORMAT. For more information on PROC FORMAT see Section 3.1 of this book.

4.3.5 SAS reporting options

System options are specifications that affect the SAS session. To specify the system options use OPTIONS statement as follows:

```
OPTIONS option(s);
```

SAS options can be inserted anywhere in a program except in data lines. These options remain in effect for the remaining of the SAS session, or until changed. For example, if only the first 100 data observations are to be used, insert the following line:

```
Options obs=100;
```

The option specified applies to the DATA or PROC step in which it is mentioned, and to all the following steps for the duration of the SAS session.

The DATASET option overrides the system option. (We looked at DATASET options in Section 3.4 of this book). For example, if the first 1000 observations of any data set are to be used except dataset *employees*, perform the following manipulations:

```
Options obs=1000;
Data annual;
Set maintenance utility employee(obs=20);
Run;
```

4.4 Generating HTML reports using ODS statements

The Output Delivery System (ODS) was introduced with version 7 as part of Base SAS (no additional software is needed in order to use ODS). The traditional SAS output has some limitations that prevent the users from obtaining the maximum value from their results. For example, the system has mono-space fonts, which do not allow the user to know in advance in what column the values of the second variable will begin in the report. ODS is designed to overcome these limitations and deliver the output in a variety of different formats, making it easy to access these outputs. After receiving data from procedures or DATA steps, ODS formats the output and the individual procedures and DATA steps do not need to format the output.

Following is an example of a program that uses ODS:

Example 4.32
```
libname a 'c:\mydata';
ods html body='odseelect-body.htm';
proc means data=a.books;
run;
ods printer close;
```

Output (notice that this output is in addition to the regular output from PROC MEANS):

```
The SAS System
The MEANS Procedur
Variable     N      Mean         Std Dev       Minimum       Maximum
cost         12     34.3708333   27.1950786    10.2500000
      99.9900000
datesold     12     14674.17     688.2402901   13880.00      15686.00
listprice    12     31.4500000   26.5468334    8.0000000
      88.9500000
```

4.4.1 The ODS statements

Different aspects of ODS can be controlled by using ODS statements.
These statements can appear anywhere in a SAS program. Some of the many different ODS statements follow:

ODS HTML
This statement opens, controls, or closes the HTML destination. Once you open the destination, HTML output can be created. To open the destination type use this line:

```
ods html body = ' destination file';
```

Close this feature by using this line:

```
ods html close;
```

You must close the HTML destination before the output can be seen with a browser.

ODS PRINTER
Opens, controls, or closes the printer destination. With the destination open, PRINTER output can be created. To open the PRINTER destination, insert the following line into the code:

```
ods printer file = 'external file';
```

If the PRINTER destination is not opened, the output will be sent to the default printer. Use this line:

```
ods printer close;
```

to close the printer feature.
The PRINTER destination must be closed before the output can be printed.

ODS TRACE
Use this statement to send the information about the output just created to the SAS log. If the line ods trace on; is inserted into the code of Example 4.32, the information about the output produced will be sent to the SAS log. This is the extra piece of information you will get in the SAS log.

```
Output Added:
-------------
Name:        Summary
Label:       Summary statistics
Template:    base.summary
Path:        Means.Summary
-------------
```

In order to stop sending information to the SAS log, use the following line to turn off the trace feature:

```
Ods trace off;
```

4.4.2 Other literature on ODS

If you would like to read more about ODS refer to *The Complete Guide to the SAS Output Delivery System, Version 8*, published by SAS institute or *Output Delivery System: The Basics*, by Lauren Haworth, published by BBU(Books by Users) of the SAS Institute.

Chapter summary

In this chapter you have seen several ways of generating reports and enhancing them using different features of SAS. You can create summary reports and frequency tables using Base SAS procedures. You can use TITLE, LABEL, FORMAT, and user-defined format statements to make your reports look better and to be more readable. You have seen how to generate HTML reports with the help of the Output Delivery System (ODS).

Now it is time to see how well you have learned the material and how much of it you have retained. So, let's look at the tests and the problems that follow. Of course, the answers and solutions follow, but first is a two–minute drill.

Two-minute drill

- Using PROC PRINT, the values of all or some of the variables can be printed.
- Using PROC PRINT, the total or subtotal of numeric variables in the dataset can be calculated.
- If the option data = is not used, PROC PRINT will print the most recently created data set.
- Some of the options of PROC PRINT are var, title, label, by, and *sum*.
- Using the var option, the values of desired variables can be printed.
- A title can be added to the output of a program by using the title option.
- To make headings more explicit, use the label option.
- To use the label, option mention the word LABEL in the first line of PROC PRINT.
- To split the label, use split = '*' in the first line of PROC PRINT.
- A label is split, but not the title.
- When using a BY statement, the PRINT procedure prints a separate analysis for each BY group.
- The sum option is used to find the total value of the variables mentioned in this statement.
- PROC REPORT can produce detailed reports and summary reports.
- If the output reports are to go to a specific dataset, mention the name of the dataset on the first line as OUT =.
- PROC REPORT produces an output by default.
- If the nowd option is not used in the PROC REPORT, a message in the log will be received saying that all subsequently submitted statements will be ignored until execution of the PROC REPORT is completed.
- The column option specifies the columns that will appear in the output.
- The summarize option writes the value of the analysis variable in the summary line.
- The compute option starts a compute block that produces a customized summary at the end of the report.
- The by option creates a separate report on a separate page for each BY group.
- A BY statement must be used with a nowd option.
- The out = option cannot be used with a BY statement.
- PROC TABULATE can produce one-, two-, or three-dimensional reports.
- To create a one-dimensional report, at least one TABLE statement is necessary.
- One, two, or three variable(s) in the TABLE statement will result in a one-, two-, or three-dimensional report.
- Variables appearing in the TABLE statement must be mentioned in the VAR or CLASS statement, but not both.
- Variables appearing in a CLASS statement can be of either character or numeric type.
- The default statistic for the variable named in the CLASS statement is N.
- The default statistic for the variable mentioned in the VAR statement is SUM.
- If statistics other than N are requested from a variable in CLASS statement, an error message will be received with no output.

- To add a statistic to a table, add an asterisks to the name of the variable in the TABLE statement.
- Space is the concatenating operator in the PROC TABULAT.
- If a variable is mentioned in a TABLE statementbut is not named it in the CLASS or VAR statement, the following error message will be received: `Type of name ( cost ) is unknown`.
- If a variable in a CLASS or a VAR statement is used and not used in the TABLE statement, the SAS system ignores it.
- Cross–tabulation of analysis variables aren't allowed.
- In a two-dimensional table, at least one variable must be included in the CLASS statement.
- Statistics cannot be requested in both the rows and the columns of the TABLE statement.
- To get the row total, add the word ALL to the end of the column part of the TABLE statement.
- To put more tables on one page or to fit one table to a page, use the `condense` option in the TABLE statement.
- The `missing` option of PROC TABULATE tells the procedure to treat missing values as a valid value in the CLASS variable.
- The syntax for the TITLE statement is `title<n><text>;`   n varies from 1 to 10.
- After a TITLE takes effect, it is used for all subsequent output until canceled or replaced.
- If two TITLE statements contain the same number, the SAS system will print the second one.
- The FOOTNOTE statement with the lowest n will appear as the highest footnote.
- If two FOOTNOTE statements contain the same number the SAS system will print the second one.
- FORMAT is a set of instructions, which tells SAS how to write an output value.
- A FORMAT is a name that contains a period.
- When using a FORMAT statement, the format is associated with the variable permanently.
- System options are specifications that affect the SAS session.
- SAS options can be inserted anywhere in a program except in data lines.
- The DATASET option overrides the SYSTEM option.
- ODS statements can appear anywhere in the program.
- The ODS HTML statement opens, controls, and closes the HTML destination.
- The HTML destination must be closed before the output can be seen with a browser.
- The ODS PRINTER statement opens, controls, or closes the PRINTER destination.
- The PRINTER destination must be closed before the output can be printed.
- Use the ODS TRACE statement to send information about the output just created to the SAS log.

Assessment exam

1. Using PROC PRINT, can the values of only some or all of the variables be printed?
2. Using the PRINT procedure, can the total values of numeric variables be calculated?
3. When using PROC PRINT, if the option `data =` is not used, what will happen?
4. If you want to print the values of only a few variables, what should you do?
5. Can a title and a label be added to PROC PRINT?
6. If you want to use LABEL in PROC PRINT, what should you do?
7. If the word `label` is not mentioned in the first line of PROC PRINT, but a LABEL statement is used in the code, what will happen?
8. How is a label split?
9. How is a title split?
10. When a BY statement is used in the PROC PRINT, what will happen?
11. What does PROC REPORT produce?
12. If the output of PROC REPORT is to go to a specific dataset, what should you do?
13. If the option NOWD is not mentioned in the first line of PROC REPORT, what will happen?
14. What is achieved when using the column option in a PROC REPORT program?
15. What is the default order of observations appearing in the output dataset?
16. How is the default order in the PROC REPORT changed?
17. In PROC REPORT, how do you specify which variable to use for providing statistics?
18. What is the type of analysis variable in PROC REPORT?
19. What is the effect of the SUMMARIZE option in the output of PROC REPORT?
20. In PROC REPORT, what does the BY statement produce?
21. Using PROC TABULATE, how many different types of reports can be produced?
22. Is it correct to say: "To create a one–dimensional report only a CLASS or a VAR statement is needed?"
23. What do we call the variable that appears in the VAR statement?
24. What is the type of the analysis variable?
25. What determines the dimension of a report?
26. When using PROC TABULATE, what happens if a character variable is used in the VAR statement?
27. Should the variable appearing in the TABLE statement be mentioned in both the VAR and CLASS statements?
28. What type of variable should appear in the CLASS statement?
29. What is the default statistic obtained for the variable named in the CLASS statement?
30. What is the default statistic obtained for the variable named in the VAR statement?
31. What happens if statistics, other than N, are requested from the variable mentioned in the CLASS statement?
32. How would you add statistics to the name of a variable in the TABLE statement?
33. What happens if a variable is mentioned in a TABLE statement but is not named in the CLASS or VAR statement?
34. What happens if a variable in a VAR or CLASS statement is mentioned but not named in the TABLE statement?
35. What is the concatenating operator in PROC TABULATE?
36. Is cross-tabulation of analysis variables allowed in PROC TABULATE?

37. Is it correct to say: "In a two–dimensional table, at least one variable must be named in the CLASS statement?"
38. What will be the result of requesting statistics in both the row and the column of the TABLE statement?
39. How would you obtain a row total in PROC TABULATE?
40. There is no need to add the key-word ALL to the CLASS statement. Why?
41. What is the difference between a 2D and 3D report?
42. How is a 3D report created?
43. How would you put more tables on one page or fit one table to a page?
44. Name the different kinds of options used to control the appearance of a report when using PROC TABULATE.
45. Name three options of PROC TABULATE.
46. What does a MISSING option do?
47. One option of PROC TABULATE is BOX= 'string'; where does this box appear on a report?
48. What does the acronym ODS stand for?
49. What is ODS designed to accomplish?
50. What do ODS statements do?
51. Where can ODS statements appear in a SAS program?
52. How is the HTML destination opened?
53. How is the HTML destination closed?
54. What happens if an ODS PRINTER statement is used in an ODS program?
55. How is information, about the output produced by ODS sent to the SAS log?

Assessment exam answers

1. All.
2. Yes.
3. PROC PRINT prints the most recently created dataset.
4. Use the VAR option.
5. Yes.
6. Mention the word label in the first line of PROC PRINT.
7. The LABEL statement will be ignored by SAS systems.
8. By using an asterisk (*).
9. No.
10. PROC PRINT prints a separate analysis for each BY group.
11. A detailed report and a summary report.
12. The dataset's name must be mentioned on the first line of PROC REPORT.
13. A message in the LOG is received saying that PROC REPORT is currently executing. All subsequently submitted statements will not begin executing until the report is completed.
14. To specify columns that will appear in the output data set.
15. Ascending.
16. By using the ORDER = option.
17. By mentioning the variable(s) in the ANALYSIS option.
18. Numeric.
19. It writes the values of analysis variables in the summary line.
20. It creates a separate report on a separate page for each BY group.

21. You can produce three different types: one-, two-, or three–dimensional report.
22. One or both are needed depending on the table being produced.
23. Analysis variable.
24. Numeric.
25. The number of commas that appear in the TABLE statement.
26. An error message is received in the LOG with no output.
27. No, it should appear in either the VAR or CLASS statement, not in both.
28. Either character or numeric.
29. The default statistic is N.
30. The default statistic is SUM.
31. An error message is received in the LOG with no output.
32. Add an asterisk to the name of the variable in the TABLE statement.
33. An error message is received saying that the type of variable is unknown.
34. SAS systems will ignore it.
35. Space.
36. No.
37. Yes.
38. An error message is received in the LOG saying that ' there are multiple statistics associated with a single cell in the following nesting…'.
39. Add the keyword ALL to the end of the column part of the TABLE statement.
40. By default, ALL is a classification variable.
41. A three–dimensional report is the same as a two–dimensional report except that it is extended over a few pages.
42. Two commas must be mentioned in the TABLE statement.
43. Add the keyword CONDENSE to the end of the TABLE statement.
44. PROC TABULATE options, options used with the TABLE statement, and systems option.
45. DATA = name of dataset, FORMAT, MISSING.
46. It tells the procedure to treat missing values as a valid value of the CLASS variable.
47. On the upper left corner.
48. Output Delivery System.
49. To overcome the limitations of traditional SAS output.
50. They manage different features of ODS.
51. Anywhere.
52. By using the following line: `ods html body = 'desination file';`.
53. By inserting the following line: `ods html close;`.
54. The output from ODS will be sent to the default printer.
55. By using the ODS trace statement.

Practice exam

1. Using PROC PRINT, which one of the following can't done?
    A. Calculating the total of some of the numeric variables
    B. Calculating the total of all the numeric values
    C. Printing some of the variables
    D. Calculating the total values of all character variables.

2. If the option DATA = is not used with a PROC PRINT, which one of the following will take place?
    A. PROC PRINT will print the most recently created dataset.
    B. If no dataset has been created in the current session of SAS, an error message is generated in the LOG with no output.
    C. Either A or B, depending on whether a dataset has been created.
    D. Neither of the above. A dataset that was created in the last session of SAS will be printed.

3. How is the LABEL option invoked with PROC PRINT?
    A. By inserting a LABEL statement in the PROC PRINT step
    B. By mentioning the word LABEL in the first line of the PROC PRINT step
    C. Both A and B
    D. Neither A nor B

4. How is a label slit?
    A. By using an asterisk in the LABEL option
    B. By mentioning the word `split` in the LABEL option
    C. By doing nothing in the LABEL option, just splitting the label where wanted
    D. It is not possible to split a label while using PROC PRINT.

5. What can a PROC REPORT produce?
    A. A detailed report
    B. A summary report
    C. Both a detailed report and a summary report
    D. Neither of the above

6. If the word NOWD is not mentioned in the first line of PROC REPORT, what will be the result?
    A. An error message will be generated in the LOG with no output.
    B. An error message will be generated in the LOG with the correct output.
    C. An error message will be generated in the LOG.
    D. None of the above.

7. When using PROC REPORT, what is the default order of the output?
    A. Descending.
    B. Ascending.
    C. Numeric variables are ascending, while character variables are descending.

D. Numeric variables are descending, while character ones are ascending.

8. What is the type of an analysis variable?
    A. Character
    B. Numeric
    C. It can be character or numeric depending on the dataset.
    D. None of the above. It is a statistical type.

9. What is the effect of the BY statement while using PROC REPORT?
    A. It creates a BY group.
    B. It creates a separate report on a separate page for each BY group.
    C. It will be ignored by PROC REPORT.
    D. It will add a title page to the beginning of the report.

10. While using PROC TABULATE, what statement is needed in order to create a one-dimensional report?
    A. A VAR statement, a CLASS statement, or both depending on the table being produced
    B. Only a VAR statement
    C. Only a CLASS statement
    D. Only a TABLE statement.

11. What is the result if a character variable is used in the VAR statement while using PROC TABULATE?
    A. Everything will be fine and you will get the output you want.
    B. You will receive an error message in the LOG with no output.
    C. You will receive an error message with the desired output.
    D. You will receive an error message with incorrect output.

12. When should the variable used in the TABLE statement be mentioned?
    A. Only in a VAR statement
    B. Only in a CLASS statement
    C. In both a VAR statement and a CLASS statement
    D. In either a VAR or CLASS statement, not in both

13. What type of variable should be named in the CLASS statement?
    A. Numeric
    B. Character
    C. A special character
    D. Either A or B

14. What is the default statistic obtained for the variable named in the CLASS statement?
    A. The default statistic is SUM.
    B. It is the *percentage* relative to the total value of the variable named in the CLASS statement.

    C. It is N.

    D. There is no default statistic for the variable mentioned in the CLASS statement.

15. What happens if a statistic other than N is requested for the variable mentioned in the CLASS statement?

    A. An error message is generated in the LOG with no output.

    B. An error message is generated with the correct output.

    C. You get correct output with no message in the LOG.

    D. Either A, B, or C.

16. Which one of the following is the concatenating operator for PROC TABULATE?

    A. An asterisk

    B. An underscore

    C. A dot

    D. A space

17. What happens if a variable in the TABLE statement is named but is not mentioned in either the VAR or CLASS statement?

    A. An error message is generated in the LOG stating that the type of variable is unknown

    B. You get the desired output with no error.

    C. SAS systems ignore that variable.

    D. None of the above.

18. What will take place if a variable in a CLASS or VAR statement is mentioned but is not named in the TABLE statement?

    A. The SAS system will ignore it.

    B. An error message will be generated in the LOG with no output.

    C. Either of A or B may take place depending on the dataset used.

    D. None of the above will take place.

19. What will be the result if statistics are requested in both row and the column of the TABLE statement of the PROC TABULATE?

    A. The SAS system will ignore all statistics and produce a default statistic.

    B. An error message will be generated with no output.

    C. The SAS system will produce all requested statistics.

    D. None of the above.

20. Is cross–tabulation of analysis variables allowed in PROC TABULATE?

    A. Yes.

    B. No.

    C. This depends on the size of the data set used.

    D. Cross–tabulation of this classification variables is allowed.

21. Which of the following will produce the row total while using PROC TABULATE?

    A. The keyword ALL will be mentioned in the row part of the TABLE statement.

    B. The keyword ALL will be mentioned in the column part of the TABLE statement.

    C. The word TOTAL will be mentioned in the row part of the TABLE statement.

D. The word TOTAL will be mentioned in the column part of the TABLE statement.

22. When using PROC TABULATE, how would you put more than one table on a page or fit one table to a page?
A. By using the keyword ALL as the PROC TABULATE option
B. By using the keyword CONDENSE at the end of the TABLE statement
C. By using the keyword CONDENSE on the same line as PROC TABULATE
D. By using the word ALL at the end of the TABLE statement

23. Which one of the following can be used in order to control the appearance of the report?
A. PROC TABULATE options
B. Options used with the TABLE statement
C. Systems options
D. All of the above

24. One option of the PROC TABULATE is BOX = 'string'. Where does the box appear in a report?
A. On the upper right corner
B. On the lower right corner
C. On the upper left corner
D. On the lower left corner

25. Which of the following lines opens the ODS destination?
A. html ods body = ' ..';
B. body = 'html ods';
C. ods html body ='..';
D. Any of the above

26. What happens if the PRINTER destination is not opened while using ODS?
A. An external file will be created by ODS.
B. An external file will not be opened by ODS.
C. ODS output will go to the SAS log.
D. ODS output will go to an external file.

27. What must you do before seeing the output sent to an ODS destination with a browser?
A. Close the HTML destination
B. Leave the HTML destination open
C. Use the ODS trace statement
D. Close the PRINTER feature

Practice exam answers

1. D
2. C
3. B
4. A
5. C

6. C
7. B
8. B
9. B
10. A
11. B
12. D
13. D
14. C
15. A
16. D
17. A
18. A
19. B
20. B
21. B
22. B
23. D
24. C
25. C
26. B
27. A

Problems

In order to learn more efficiently, please try to solve these problems before looking at the solutions at the end of the chapter.

1. You have a dataset called BOOKS that contains variables AUTHOR, TITLE, PUBLISHER, COST, and PRICE. Write a program to produce a report listing the following variables in the given order: PUBLISHER, AUTHOR, PRICE (use DOLLAR7.2 format). Here is a sample of the data to work with:

AUTHOR	TITLE	COST	PRICE
J_Miller	Algebra	$12.99	$14.99
A_Green	Cars	$9.95	$11.49
B_White	Science	$23.99	$25.99
J_Wilson	Horses	$39.95	$44.99
K_Cool	Herbs	$11.39	$12.99

2. Use the dataset of problem 4.1 to write code to produce a report that includes the sum of each of the variables *cost* and *price*, a title, and comma format.

3. Use the data of problem 1 to write code to produce a report, which contains the sum of the variable *price* for each *author*; each variable in the output dataset will have a descriptive label.

4. Use the following dataset, which is called EMPLOYEE and has the following variables: L_NAME, SS_NUM, INCOME, TAX. Write code using PROC REPORT to produce a simple report, that includes the variables L_NAME and TAX only for those employees whose TAX is less than $5000. Make sure you use the right option so that the subsequent SAS statements do not have to wait until execution of the PROC REPORT is completed.

L_NAME	SS_NUM	INCOME	TAX
Jones	222333444	45000	4500
White	121234345	79000	6800
White	121234345	29000	1900
Dodd	998899112	66500	5950
Dodd	998899112	17000	182

5. Use the dataset of problem 4 to write a program that sums up the variable INCOME for each employee and summarizes the result for each one. To make the report more readable, skip a line before each line of summary.

6. You are given the dataset of problem 4. Use PROC TABULATE to write a program that produces a table with one column.

7. Using the dataset of problem 4 write a program that produces a two–dimensional report with the variable L_NAME as the row and INCOME as the column.

8. Repeat problem 7 but also calculate the mean of the variable INCOME for each employee.

9. Use the dataset of problem 4 to write code, that produces a two–dimensional table with the row designated as the name of the employee and two columns with mean income as the first column and mean tax as the second.

10. Use the data set of problem 4 to write code, that produces a two–dimensional table with the row designated as the name of the employees and the first column as income and the second one as tax. Calculate the sum of income and tax.

Problem solutions

1.
```
Proc print data=BOOKS;
Var PUBLISHER AUTHOR PRICE;
Format PRICE dollar7.2;
Run;
```

2.
```
proc print data=BOOKS;
var AUTHOR COST PRICE;
sum COST PRICE;
format COST PRICE comma8.2;
title 'This a Brief Report';
run;
```

3. (Remember that the dataset must be sorted beforehand in order to use the BY statement.)
```
proc print data = BOOKS label;
var AUTHOR COST PRICE;
sum PRICE;
by AUTHOR;
label AUTHOR = 'Name of Author'
COST = 'Cost of the Book'
PRICE = 'Price of the Book';
run;
```

4.
```
proc report data = EMPLOYEE nowd;
column L_NAME TAX;
where TAX lt 5000;
run;
```

5. In the following program, note the options OL and SKIP:
```
proc report data = EMPLOYEE nowd;
define L_NAME / order;
define INCOME / analysis sum;
break after L_NAME / ol summarize skip;
run;
```

6.
```
proc tabulate data=EMPLOYEE;
var INCOME TAX;
class L_NAME;
table L_NAME:
```

```
    run;

7.  proc tabulate data=EMPLOYEE;
    var INCOME TAX;
    class L_NAME;
    table L_NAME , INCOME:
    run;

8.  proc tabulate data=EMPLOYEE;
    var INCOME TAX;
    class L_NAME;
    table L_NAME , INCOME*mean:
    run;

9.  proc tabulate data=EMPLOYEE;
    var INCOME TAX;
    class L_NAME;
    table L_NAME , INCOME*mean TAX*mean:
    run;

10. proc tabulate data=EMPLOYEE;
    var INCOME TAX;
    class L_NAME;
    table L_NAME all , INCOME TAX:
    run;
```

5 Handling Errors

Certification objectives

In this chapter you will learn what you need in order to pass the section of the exam, including

- **Recognizing and correcting syntax errors**
- **Identifying and correcting semantic errors**
- **Examining and resolving execution–time errors**
- **Identifying and correcting data errors**
- **Examining and resolving macro-related errors**
- **Identifying and resolving programming logic errors**

As you probably already know, when a SAS program is executed, SAS generates different messages about the dataset created and about errors found in the program. SAS performs error processing during the compilation phase as well as the execution phase. All messages produced are sent to the SAS log. If you read and understand the SAS log, you should be able to debug your SAS program.

Different methods and tools are used for debugging a SAS program. For example, logic errors can be detected by using the SAS DATA step debugger.

We will look at the various types of error, listed below, that may occur in a SAS program and investigate different ways to prevent, detect, and correct them:

1. Syntax errors
2. Semantic errors
3. Execution–time errors
4. Data error
5. Macro-related errors
6. Logic errors

5.1 Recognizing and correcting Syntax errors

A syntax error occurs when program statements do not conform to the rules of the SAS language.

Common syntax errors include misspelling a SAS keyword, using unmatched quotation marks, forgetting a semicolon, and specifying an invalid statement option or an invalid dataset option.

When SAS finds a syntax error, it tries to correct it and will send a message to the log mentioning the action taken. If unsuccessful, SAS stops processing the step and sends an error message to the log beginning with the word ERROR along with an explanation of the error and its possible location.

We will going to look at a few examples.

Example 5.1
In this program the keyword DATA is misspelled DAT. SAS is able to identify the error and correct it. SAS sends a warning message to the log beginning with the word WARNING.

```
dat a;
idnum=123;
run;
```

Log:

```
1    dat a;
     ---
     14
WARNING 14-169: Assuming the symbol DATA was misspelled as dat.
2    idnum=123;
3    run;
NOTE: The data set WORK.A has 1 observations and 1 variables.
NOTE: DATA statement used:
     real time            0.76 seconds
```

In the next example all keywords are spelled properly but a semicolon is left out. SAS is unable to correct the problem, so it issues an error message in the log beginning with the word ERROR. SAS stops processing the DATA step. Whether it can execute the subsequent steps depends on (1) which method of running SAS you are using or (2) your operating environment.

Example 5.2
```
data a
idnum=123;
run;
```

Log:

```
7    data a
NOTE: SCL source line.
8    idnum=123;
          -
          22
          76
ERROR 22-322: Syntax error, expecting one of the following: a name, a quoted
string, (, /, ;,
               _DATA_, _LAST_, _NULL_.
ERROR 76-322: Syntax error, statement will be ignored.
9    run;
NOTE: The SAS System stopped processing this step because of errors.
NOTE: DATA statement used:
     real time            0.04 seconds
```

The following example has a syntax error in a PROC step. SAS can identify the error and correct it. It sends a message to the log and generates the correct output.

Example 5.3
```
libname a 'c:\mydata';
pro means data =a.books;
run;
```

Log:

```
25    libname a 'c:\mydata';
NOTE: Libref A was successfully assigned as follows:
      Engine:         V8
      Physical Name: c:\mydata
NOTE: SCL source line.
26    pro means data =a.books;
      ---
      14
WARNING 14-169: Assuming the symbol PROC was misspelled as pro.
27    run;
NOTE: There were 9 observations read from the data set A.BOOKS.
NOTE: PROCEDURE MEANS used:
      real time              0.49 seconds
```

In the following example SAS can't correct the problem in the PROC step, so it sends a message to the log and stops processing the step.

Example 5.4

```
libname a 'c:\mydata';
proc means data =a.books noss;
run;
```

Log:

```
31    libname a 'c:\mydata';
NOTE: Libref A was successfully assigned as follows:
      Engine:         V8
      Physical Name: c:\mydata
NOTE: SCL source line.
32    proc means data =a.books noss;
                              -----
                              22    200
ERROR 22-322: Syntax error, expecting one of the following: ;, (, ALPHA,
CHARTYPE, CLASSDATA,
              CLM, COMPLETETYPES, CSS, CV, DATA, DESCEND, DESCENDING,
DESCENDTYPES, EXCLNPWGT,
              EXCLNPWGTS, EXCLUSIVE, FW, IDMIN, KURTOSIS, LCLM, MAX, MAXDEC,
MEAN, MEDIAN, MIN,
              MISSING, N, NDEC, NMISS, NONOBS, NOPRINT, NOTRAP, NWAY, ORDER,
P1, P10, P25, P5,
              P50, P75, P90, P95, P99, PCTLDEF, PRINT, PRINTALL, PRINTALLTYPES,
PRINTIDS,
              PRINTIDVARS, PROBT, Q1, Q3, QMARKERS, QMETHOD, QNTLDEF, QRANGE,
RANGE, SKEWNESS,
              STDDEV, STDERR, SUM, SUMSIZE, SUMWGT, T, UCLM, USS, VAR, VARDEF.
ERROR 200-322: The symbol is not recognized and will be ignored.
33    run;
NOTE: The SAS System stopped processing this step because of errors.
NOTE: PROCEDURE MEANS used:
      real time              0.00 seconds
```

The problem is that the option noss is spelled incorrectly.

TIP: In order to solve this problem, option noss should be correctly spelled nos. What happens if all SAS statements are correct, but they are not valid for the intended usage? We'll learn the answer in the next section.

5.2 Identifying and correcting Semantic errors

A semantic error occurs when the SAS statement is correct but the elements are not valid for that usage.

Some examples of semantic errors are: in a DATA step `libref` has not been previously assigned in a LIBNAME statement, using a numeric variable name where only a character variable is valid, or specifying the wrong number of arguments for a function.

We are going to look at some examples.

In the following example the `libref` NEW has not been previously assigned in a LIBNAME statement.

Example 5.5
```
data b;
set new.employee;
run;
```

Log:

```
1    data b;
2    set new.employee;
ERROR: Libname NEW is not assigned.
3    run;
NOTE: The SAS System stopped processing this step because of errors.
WARNING: The data set WORK.B may be incomplete.  when this step was stopped
there were 0
          observations and 0 variables.
NOTE: DATA statement used:
      real time          0.50 seconds
```

TIP: In order to remove the error, insert the following line of code at the beginning of the program: `libname new 'address of the file';`

In the next example an illegal reference to the array Y has been detected by SAS.

Example 5.6
```
data a;
array y(*)y1-y3;
y=5;
cards;
1 2
3 4
5 6
7 8
;
run;
```

Log:
```
4     data a;
5     array y(*)y1-y3;
6     y=5;
ERROR: Illegal reference to the array y.
7     cards;
NOTE: The SAS System stopped processing this step because of errors.
WARNING: The data set WORK.A may be incomplete.  When this step was stopped
there were 0
          observations and 3 variables.
NOTE: DATA statement used:
      real time            0.22 seconds
```

TIP: In order to solve this problem, remove the line y=5; .

In the next example, the names of the dataset in the DATA step and in the output statement are not the same.

Example 5.7
```
data a;
input idnum ;
cards;
1
2
3
4
5
6
;
run;

data abc;
set a;
if idnum > 3 then output ab;
run;
```

Log:

```
42    data a;
43    input idnum ;
44    cards;
NOTE: The data set WORK.A has 6 observations and 1 variables.
NOTE: DATA statement used:
      real time            0.06 seconds
51    ;
52    run;
53    data abc;
54    set a;
NOTE: SCL source line.
55    if idnum > 3 then output ab;
                                --
                               455
ERROR 455-185: Data set was not specified on the DATA statement.
56    run;
NOTE: The SAS System stopped processing this step because of errors.
```

```
WARNING: The data set WORK.ABC may be incomplete.  When this step was stopped
there were 0
        observations and 1 variables.
WARNING: Data set WORK.ABC was not replaced because this step was stopped.
NOTE: DATA statement used:
      real time            0.05 seconds
```

TIP: In order to solve this problem, change the name of the dataset in the output statement to abc, so that the line of code becomes
```
if idnum > 3 then output abc;
```

5.3 Examining and resolving execution–time errors

Execution–time errors take place when SAS applies compiled programs to data values. When SAS detects this type of error, it usually generates a warning or a note and continues to process the program.

Some common execution–time errors are illegal mathematical operations such as division by zero, illegal arguments to functions, or observations in the wrong order in the BY group processing.

Another execution–time error occurs when an out–of–resources condition is encountered, such as insufficient memory or a full disk. When this condition occurs SAS will try to free up some memory space and will ask you for permission to delete temporary datasets. This seldom occurs.

We will look at some execution–time errors by considering several examples.

In the following example a division by zero is taking place, that produces an execution–time error. SAS executes the entire step and assigns a missing value for the variable cost in the third line of data in the output.

Example 5.8
```
data invet;
input totcost numperch;
cost=totcost/numperch;
datalines;
250 25
420 10
565 0
899 25
;
run;
```

Log:

```
78    data invet;
79    input totcost numperch;
80    cost=totcost/numperch;
81    datalines;
NOTE: Division by zero detected at line 80 column 13.
RULE:       ----+----1----+----2----+----3----+----4----+----5----+----6----+---
-7----+----8----+---
84         565 0
totcost=565 numperch=0 cost=. _ERROR_=1 _N_=3
```

```
NOTE: Mathematical operations could not be performed at the following places.
The results of the
      operations have been set to missing values.
      Each place is given by: (Number of times) at (Line):(Column).
      1 at 80:13
NOTE: The data set WORK.INVET has 4 observations and 3 variables.
NOTE: DATA statement used:
      real time          0.11 seconds
86    ;
87    run;
```

Output:

```
The SAS System              09:47 Tuesday, June 8, 2004   2
                            Obs     totcost    numperch      cost
                             1        250         25        10.00
                             2        420         10        42.00
                             3        565          0          .
                             4        899         25        35.96
```

TIP: This error can be avoided by calculating the value of the variable cost *when variable* numperch *is greater than zero. The following IF statement will do the job:*
```
If numperch > 0 then cost = totcost/numperch;
```

In the following example, the semicolon at the end of the TITLE statement is missing. Because of the position of the TITLE statement in the program, the CLASS statement becomes part of the TITLE statement. SAS will continue processing the program and may produce an unwanted result. A warning message has been sent to the log saying that there may be something wrong with the TITLE statement.

Example 5.9
```
libname a 'c:\mydata';
proc means data=a.books;
title 'Analysis of the books at hand'
class author;
var cost;
run;
```

Log:

```
100   libname a 'c:\mydata';
NOTE: Libref A was successfully assigned as follows:
      Engine:      V8
      Physical Name: c:\mydata
101   proc means data=a.books;
102   title 'Analysis of the books at hand'
103   class suthor;
WARNING: The TITLE statement is ambiguous due to invalid options or unquoted
text.
104   var cost;
105   run;
NOTE: There were 9 observations read from the data set A.BOOKS.
```

```
NOTE: PROCEDURE MEANS used:
      real time           0.05 seconds
```
Output:

```
The SAS System                09:47 Tuesday, June 8, 2004
                         The MEANS Procedure
   Variable      N        Mean        Std Dev      Minimum     Maximum

   cost          9    25.9466667    14.7143518   10.2500000  51.5000000
   datesold      9    14063.89     129.4656754   13880.00    14225.00
   listprice     9    22.4966667    13.2760367    8.0000000  45.9900000
```

In the following example SAS detects an execution–time error and stops processing. The program processes an array, and SAS encounters an out-of-range value for the array's subscript and stops processing.

Example 5.10

```
data cde;
array x(*) x1 - x3;
input n idnum;
if idnum > 0 then x(n) = idnum;
datalines;
1 2
3 4
5 6
;
run;
proc print data=cde;
run;
```

Log:

```
142   data cde;
143   array x(*) x1-x3;
144   input n idnum;
145   if idnum > 0 then x(n) = idnum;
146   datalines;
ERROR: Array subscript out of range at line 145 column 19.
RULE:     ----+----1----+----2----+----3----+----4----+----5----+----6----+---
-7----+----8----+---
149       5 6
x1=. x2=. x3=. n=5 idnum=6 _ERROR_=1 _N_=3
NOTE: The SAS System stopped processing this step because of errors.
WARNING: The data set WORK.CDE may be incomplete.  When this step was stopped
there were 2
         observations and 5 variables.
WARNING: Data set WORK.CDE was not replaced because this step was stopped.
NOTE: DATA statement used:
      real time           0.04 seconds
150   ;
151   run;
152   proc print data=cde;
153   run;
NOTE: No observations in data set WORK.CDE.
```

```
NOTE: PROCEDURE PRINT used:
      real time              0.00 seconds
```

TIP: You can avoid this error by changing the line `array x(*)   x1 - x3;` *to* `array x(*)   x1 - x5;`

5.4 Identifying and correcting data errors

A data error occurs when a data value is not appropriate for the SAS program that you have written. These errors are detected by SAS during execution of the program, but they are different from execution–time errors. With execution–time errors something is wrong in the program statements, but with data errors, the data values are wrong. For example, if a data value that you have defined to be numeric is actually character, then SAS will generate a data error.

When SAS detects the data error during execution of the program, it sends a note to the log explaining the problem and sets _ERROR_ to one for the current observation. SAS continues to process the program.

We will study some examples. In the first example, the value of the numeric type variable income is written as a character because of the dollar sign in line 3.

Example 5.11
```
data a ;
input name $ income;
datalines;
jone 45000
jane 33000
bob  $80000
george 40000
;
run;
proc print data=a;
run;
```

Log:

```
1     data a ;
2     input name $ income;
3     datalines;
NOTE: Invalid data for income in line 6 6-11.
RULE:        ----+----1----+----2----+----3----+----4----+----5----+----6----+---
-7----+----8----+---
6          bob  $80000
name=bob income=. _ERROR_=1 _N_=3
NOTE: The data set WORK.A has 4 observations and 2 variables.
NOTE: DATA statement used:
      real time              0.83 seconds
8     ;
9     run;
10    proc print data=a;
11    run;
NOTE: There were 4 observations read from the data set WORK.A.
NOTE: PROCEDURE PRINT used:
```

```
real time          0.50 seconds
```

Output:

Obs	name	income			
			1	jone	
45000					
			2	jane	
33000					
			3	bob	
.					

In the next example the number of days for a month is typed as 32, while the maximum number of days in a month is 31.

Example 5.12
```
data date ;
input name $ bdate mmddyy10.;;
datalines;
jone 020199
jane 083297
bob  010101
george 092298
;
run;
proc print data=date;
format bdate mmddyy10.;
run;
```

Log:

```
12    data date ;
13    input name $ bdate mmddyy10.;;
14    datalines;
NOTE: Invalid data for bdate in line 16 6-15.
RULE:     ----+----1----+----2----+----3----+----4----+----5----+----6----+---
-7----+----8----+---
16          jane 0832
name=jane bdate=. _ERROR_=1 _N_=2
NOTE: The data set WORK.DATE has 4 observations and 2 variables.
NOTE: DATA statement used:
      real time          0.16 seconds
19    ;
20    run;
21    proc print data=date;
22    format bdate mmddyy10.;
23    run;
NOTE: There were 4 observations read from the data set WORK.DATE.
NOTE: PROCEDURE PRINT used:
      real time          0.10 seconds
```

Output:

obs	name	bdate		
02/01/1999			1	jone
.			2	jane
01/01/2001			3	bob

5.5 Examining and resolving macro-related errors

The SAS macro facility is a tool for text substitution and is a component of Base SAS. If you have access to the SAS systems, you have access to the macro facility and can include macro facility features in your program.

Macro is not part of the *Base SAS certification exam*. Since the primary objective of this text is to help the reader pass (the exam), we will not focus on macro or macro–related errors. However, briefly speaking; there are several types of macro–related errors: macro compile-time and macro execution–time errors, errors in SAS code produced by the macro facility.

If you would like to read more about macros, please consult *SAS Macro Language: Reference.*

For more examples on macros, you can consult SAS Macro Programming Made Easy by Michele M. Burlew.

5.6 Identifying and resolving programming logic errors

You sometimes may experience a logic error in your program when the program has compiled and executed with no problem whatsoever. You review the SAS log and find no error message. But when you review the result of the program, it is not what it should be. You have a logic error in your program when your program seems to do everything correctly, but does not produce the desired result.

The following example shows a very simple logic error. The program is intended to print the name of people who have obtained a bonus of more than 10000 in the month of June, but since no dataset is provided for the PROC PRINT statement, PROC PRINT will use the latest dataset created, which is for the month of July.

Example 5.13
```
data junebonu;
input f_name $ l_name $ salary bonus;
datalines;
john davis 65000 12000
jane volk 71000 9000
fred gains 59000 8000
rohnda steeves 81000 11000
;
run;
```

```
data julybonu;
input f_name $ l_name $ salary bonus;
datalines;
georige paterson 45000 5000
ron miler 55000 1000
tom jones 44000 13000
brian smith 89000 14000
;
run;


proc print;
where bonus > 10000;
run;
```

Notice that the program has no error and SAS does not show any in the log. But the note from PROC PRINT shows that the output generated is from data for the month of July.

Log:

```
43    data junebonu;
44    input f_name $ l_name $ salary bonus;
45    datalines;
NOTE: The data set WORK.JUNEBONU has 4 observations and 4 variables.
NOTE: DATA statement used:
      real time           0.05 seconds
      cpu time            0.05 seconds
50    ;
51    run;
52    data julybonu;
53    input f_name $ l_name $ salary bonus;
54    datalines;
NOTE: The data set WORK.JULYBONU has 4 observations and 4 variables.
NOTE: DATA statement used:
      real time           0.04 seconds
      cpu time            0.04 seconds
59    ;
60    run;
61    proc print;
62    where bonus > 10000;
63    run;
NOTE: There were 2 observations read from the data set WORK.JULYBONU.
      WHERE bonus>10000;
NOTE: PROCEDURE PRINT used:
      real time           0.01 seconds
      cpu time            0.01 seconds
```

How can you determine whether there is a logic error in your program? A good way is to copy a few lines of the DATA step into another DATA step, execute it, and carefully inspect the result of these statements to see if you get what you were expecting. A second way is to read the SAS log carefully and look for any unusual messages. The third is to use one of the tools that SAS provides to detect logic errors. Two of the tools SAS provides to find logic errors are

1. DATA step debugger

2. PUT statement

We will consider these tools briefly and provide you with reference for further consultation.

5.6.1 DATA step debugger

DATA step debugger can be used to find logic errors and some data errors. It is an interactive component of SAS, which consists of windows and a group of commands. Through issuing commands, you can execute DATA step statements and stop to look at the results in a window.

By looking at variables' values in the window, you can see where the logic error is taking place. Since the DATA step debugger is an interactive tool, you can repeat this process as many times as you want in a single session of debugging.

To invoke the debugger, just add the DEBUG option to DATA step and run the program.

TIP: *Remember that the debugger is for DATA step only. If used for a PROC step, a syntax error will be generated with no output.*

The next example shows how to start a debugging session and lists the contents of the debugger source window. The DEBUG option is added to a program of one of the previous examples.

Example 5.14
```
data julybonu/debug;
input f_name $ l_name $ salary bonus;
datalines;
georige paterson 45000 5000
ron miler 55000 1000
tom jones 44000 13000
brian smith 89000 14000
;
run;
```

The DEBUGGER SOURCE window shows the DATA step code as it appears in the SAS log. Notice that the lines of the program have the same number as do the ones in the SAS log. The DEBUGGER SOURCE window highlights the next line to be executed.

```
94 data julybonu/debug;
   95 input f_name $ l_name $ salary bonus;
   96 datalines;
```

Some of the tasks that can be performed using DATA step debugger are

1. Executing statements one by one or in groups
2. Bypassing execution of one or several statements

3. Displaying the values of variables and assigning new values to them

4. Monitoring the values of variables and suspending the execution of the program at the point where a value changes

5.6.2 PUT statement

The PUT statement writes information to the SAS log, to the SAS procedure output, or to an external file. There are different ways to write a PUT statement.

To read more about the PUT statement, please refer to the *Language Reference: Dictionary, Version 8.*

In order to debug a program, use a PUT statement to write the variables' values and other messages to the SAS log.

The following example shows how to use the PUT statement to write information about different observations in the DATA step. The program considers two kinds of information: employee information and bonus information. The program executes with no error message in the log, but the output is not correct because the employee information is not retained with the bonus data.

Example 5.15
```
data julbonus;
input @1 type $1. @;
if type='e' then do;
input @3 empno 2. +1 fname $3. +1 lname $5. +1 salary 5.;
end;
else if type='b' then do;
input bonus $5.;
output;
end;
datalines;
e 12 pit jones 45000
b $4000
b $1000
e 34 bob woody 56000
b $5000
run;
proc print data=julbonus;
run;
```

Notice that there is no error message in the log.

Log:

```
421   data julbonus;
422   input @1 type $1. @;
423   if type='e' then do;
424   input @3 empno 2. +1 fname $3. +1 lname $5. +1 salary 5.;
425   end;
426   else if type='b' then do;
427   input bonus $5.;
428   output;
```

```
429   end;
430   datalines;
NOTE: The data set WORK.JULBONUS has 3 observations and 6 variables.
NOTE: DATA statement used:
      real time              0.05 seconds
436   run;
437   proc print data=julbonus;
438   run;
NOTE: There were 3 observations read from the data set WORK.JULBONUS.
NOTE: PROCEDURE PRINT used:
      real time              0.05 seconds
```

Notice that the output dataset does not have the employee information.

Output:

The SAS System		11:56 Sunday, June 13, 2004 21				
bonus	Obs	type	empno	fname	lname	salary
$400	1	b	.			.
$100	2	b	.			.
$500	3	b	.			.

Now, add a PUT statement after each INPUT statement in order to see that the information about each employee is not retained for all iterations of the DATA step. The modified program is as follows:

```
data julbonus;
input @1 type $1. @;
if type='e' then do;
input @3 empno 2. +1 fname $3. +1 lname $5. +1 salary 5.;
put 'empl info:'empno= fname= lname= salary=;
end;
else if type='b' then do;
input bonus $5.;
put 'empl bonus:' empno= fname= lname= bonus= ;
output;
end;
datalines;
e 12 pit jones 45000
b $4000
b $1000
e 34 bob woody 56000
b $5000
run;
proc print data=julbonus;
run;
```

Log:

```
380   data julbonus;
381   input @1 type $1. @;
382   if type='e' then do;
383   input @3 empno 2. +1 fname $3. +1 lname $5. +1 salary 5.;
384   put 'empl info:'empno= fname= lname= salary=;
385   end;
386   else if type='b' then do;
387   input bonus $5.;
388   put 'empl bonus:' empno= fname= lname= bonus= ;
389   output;
390   end;
391   datalines;
empl info:empno=12 fname=pit lname=jones salary=45000
empl bonus:empno=. fname=   lname=   bonus=$400
empl bonus:empno=. fname=   lname=   bonus=$100
empl info:empno=34 fname=bob lname=woody salary=56000
empl bonus:empno=. fname=   lname=   bonus=$500
NOTE: The data set WORK.JULBONUS has 3 observations and 6 variables.
NOTE: DATA statement used:
      real time              0.04 seconds
397   run;
398   proc print data=julbonus;
399   run;
NOTE: There were 3 observations read from the data set WORK.JULBONUS.
NOTE: PROCEDURE PRINT used:
      real time              0.05 seconds
```

To solve the problem, add a RETAIN statement to the program to retain the information about the employee across the iterations of the DATA step.

```
data julbonus;
input @1 type $1. @;
if type='e' then do;
input @3 empno 2. +1 fname $3. +1 lname $5. +1 salary 5.;
end;
retain empno fname lname salary;
else if type='b' then do;
input bonus $5.;
output;
end;
datalines;
e 12 pit jones 45000
b $4000
b $1000
e 34 bob woody 56000
b $5000
run;
proc print data=julbonus;
run;
```

The output after the RETAIN statement is added, and the output dataset now has all the necessary information.

Output:

The SAS System	11:56 Sunday, June 13, 2004 20					
bonus	Obs	type	empno	fname	lname	salary
$400	1	b	12	pit	jones	45000
$100	2	b	12	pit	jones	45000
	3	b	34	bob	woody	56000

To read more about SAS DEBUGGER, PUT statement, and other SAS tools used to detect logic errors, please refer to chapter 3 and 4 of *Debugging SAS Program, a Handbook of Tools and Techniques,* by *Michele M. Burlew.*

Chapter summary

In this chapter we looked at different types of errors, that may occur during compilation or execution of a SAS program. We looked at different ways to prevent, detect, and correct errors, and also at some tools that SAS provides for detection of SAS program logic errors.

Two-minute drill

- Syntax errors occur when program statements do not conform to the rules of the SAS language.
- Some common syntax errors are misspelling a SAS keyword, or unmatched quotation marks.
- If SAS can't correct a syntax error, the system will send a message to the log beginning with the word ERROR.
- A semantic error occurs when the SAS statement is correct but the elements are not valid for the intended usage.
- Some examples of semantic error are the omission of libref assignment in a LIBNAME statement or using a numeric variable name where only a character variable is valid.
- An execution–time error occurs when SAS applies compiled programs to data values and the results are incorrect.
- When SAS detects an execution–time error, it usually generates a warning or a note and continues to process the program.
- Some common execution–time errors are illegal mathematical operations such as division by zero, or illegal arguments to a function.
- An out–of–resource condition also creates an execution–time error.
- A data error occurs when a data value is not appropriate for the SAS program written.
- Data errors are detected during execution of the program, but they differ from execution–time errors.
- An example of a data error is a data value that is defined to be numeric but is actually a character value.
- When SAS detects the data error, it sends a note to the log explaining the problem and sets _ERROR_ to one for the current observation.
- A programming logic error occurs if the program compiles and executes properly but the result is incorrect.
- One way to find a logic error in your program is to inspect the data and the output of the program, read the SAS log carefully and look for unusual messages, or use one of the tools provided by SAS such as DATA step debugger or the PUT statement.
- If you use the debugger in a PROC step, a syntax error will result.

Assessment exam

1. When does a syntax error occur?
2. Name two common syntax errors that were mentioned in the text.
3. What does SAS do on finding a syntax error?
4. If a semicolon is left out in a DATA step, what is the most likely error to take place?
5. When SAS finds an error in a step, will the subsequent steps be processed automatically?
6. What kind of error will occur if all SAS statements are correct but are not valid for the intended usage?
7. Name two of the common semantic errors mentioned in the text.
8. If the wrong number of arguments is specified for a function, what kind of error will occur?
9. When does an execution–time error occur?
10. When SAS detects an execution–time error, what kind of action does it take?
11. Name two common execution–time errors mentioned in the text.
12. If an illegal mathematical operation such as division by zero takes place, what kind of error will occur?
13. If an out–of–resources condition takes place, what kind of error will occur?
14. If an out–of–resources condition takes place, what is the first action that SAS will take?
15. If a data value is not appropriate for the SAS program, what kind of error will occur?
16. When are data errors detected by SAS?
17. When does a data error occur?
18. Does SAS detect data errors during compilation of the program?
19. What is the difference between a data error and an execution–time error?
20. What is an example of a data error?
21. What action does SAS take after detecting a data error?
22. How would you know if there is a logic error in your program?
23. What is a good way to determine whether there is a logic error in the program?
24. Name two of the tools SAS provides to detect logic errors.
25. What does the DATA step debugger consist of?
26. Using the DATA step debugger, how can you detect logic errors?
27. In a single session of debugging, how many times can you use the DATA step debugger?
28. How would you invoke the debugger?
29. Is it possible to use the debugger in a PROC step? If you do, what will be the result?
30. What does the PUT statement do?
31. How would you use the PUT statement to debug a program?

Assessment exam answers

1. When program statements do not conform to the rules of SAS language.
2. Misspelling a SAS keyword, using unmatched quotation marks.
3. It tries to correct the problem and if it does not succeed, it stops processing and will send an error message to the log beginning with the word ERROR.
4. A syntax error is most likely to take place.
5. No. Whether SAS can execute the subsequent steps depends on which method of SAS is used and also on the operating environment.
6. A semantic error will take place.

7. Two common semantic errors occur when (a) in a DATA step, `libref` has not been previously assigned in a LIBNAME statementand (b) a numeric variable name has been used where only a character variable is valid.
8. A semantic error will occur.
9. When SAS applies compiled programs to data values.
10. It generates a warning or a note and continues to process the program.
11. Illegal argument to functions; observations in wrong order in the BY group processing.
12. An execution–time error will occur.
13. An execution–time error will occur.
14. It will try to free up some memory and will send you a note to ask for your permission.
15. A data error will take place.
16. During execution of the program.
17. A data error occurs when a data value is not appropriate for the SAS program.
18. No. SAS detects data errors during the execution time of the program.
19. With the execution–time error something is wrong with the program statements, while with data errors data values are wrong.
20. An example is a data value defined to be numeric but that is actually character.
21. SAS sends a note to the log explaining the problem and sets _ERROR_ to one for the current observation. SAS will continue to process the program.
22. When the program compiles and executes correctly but the output is not what was expected.
23. A good way is to copy a few lines of the DATA step into another DATA step, execute it, and carefully inspect the result to see if you get what was expected.
24. One is the DATA step debugger; the other is the PUT statement.
25. It is an interactive component of SAS and consists of windows and a group of commands.
26. Through issuing commands you can execute DATA step statements and stop to look at results in a window.
27. Since the DATA step debugger is an interactive tool, you can use it as many times as you want in a single session of debugging.
28. Just add the DEBUG option to the DATA step.
29. No. If you do, you will get a syntax error.
30. It writes information to the SAS log.
31. By writing variable values and other messages to the SAS log.

Practice exam

1. A syntax error occurs when
   A. Statements are correct but the elements are not valid for that usage
   B. Program statements do not conform to the rules of the SAS language
   C. An out-of-resources condition takes place
   D. A data value is not appropriate for the SAS program that is executing

2. When a SAS keyword is misspelled, which type of error takes place?
   A. Semantic
   B. Data
   C. Syntax
   D. Logic

3. What type of error will the following program produce?
   ```
   Data salary
   Id = 234;
   Run;
   ```
   A. Semantic
   B. Syntax
   C. Either
   D. Neither

4. If a syntax error occurs and SAS can't correct the problem, what will happen?
   A. SAS stops processing the program.
   B. SAS will send a warning message to the log.
   C. SAS will send an error message to the log explaining the problem.
   D. SAS will stop processing the program and will send an error message to the log beginning with the word ERROR.

5. What is the result of running the following program?
   ```
   Data b
   Input name $;
   Dataline;
   Abc
   Def
   ;
   ```

```
ru;
```

SAS will

A. Detect the problem, correct it, and send a note to the log explaining the action taken
B. Produce a syntax error and stop processing the program
C. Produce a syntax error and continues, processing the program since the program is short
D. Execute this step, but will not run the next step.

6. If you run this program, what will be the outcome?

```
Libname a 'c:\mydata';
Pro means data = a.books;
Run;
```

A. SAS detects the problem, corrects it, and will send a warning message to the log explaining the problem and the action taken.
B. SAS will correct the problem and send an error message to the log stating that a syntax error was detected.
C. SAS will correct the problem and send both a warning and an error message to the log.
D. SAS can't compile the program and will stop processing it.

7. What is the result of running the following program?

```
Libname   abc 'c:\mydata';
Proc means data=abc.book noss;
Run;
```

A. SAS will correct the problem and send a message to the log explaining the action taken and continue to process the program.
B. A syntax error will be detected, an error message will be sent to the log, and SAS will stop processing the program.
C. No problem will be detected, and SAS will successfully compile and execute the program.
D. SAS will compile the program correctly, but will not be able to execute it.

8. A semantic error occurs when

A. There is an error in the data.
B. One of the options of the DATA step is not spelled correctly.
C. SAS statements are correct but the elements are not valid for that usage.
D. Invalid mathematical operation takes place.

9. What is the result of running the following program?

```
Data bb;
Set ab.employee;
Run;
```

A. No problem will be detected; the program will compile and execute.
B. A syntax error will be detected and SAS will stop processing the program.
C. A semantic error will be detected; SAS will correct the problem, send a note to the log explaining the problem, and continue processing the program.

D. A semantic error will be detected and SAS will stop processing the program and will send an error message to the log.

10. In the previous problem what action should you take to remedy the situation?
    A. Change the name of the dataset in the first line of DATA step to 'ab'.
    B. Insert the following line of code: libname ab 'address of the file'.
    C. Insert the following line of code: libname bb 'address of the file'.
    D. No action is needed since there is no error in the program.

11. What is the result of running the following program?
```
Data cd;
Array y(*) y1-y6;
Y=9;
Datalines;
10 20
30 40
50 60
70 80
;
run;
```
    A. The program will compile and execute with no problem.
    B. A syntax error will occur and SAS will stop processing the program.
    C. A semantic error will be detected and SAS will stop processing this step.
    D. SAS will process the program and will send a warning to the log, mentioning that the dataset 'cd' may be incomplete.

12. How would you correct the situation in the previous problem?
    A. Add a LIBNAME statement to the beginning of the program.
    B. Remove the asterisk in the dimension of the array.
    C. Remove the line: y=9;.
    D. Change the name of the array.

13. If you run the following program, what will be the result?
```
Data emplid;
Input idnum;
Datalines;
101
201
301
401
501
;
run;

data depart;
set emplid;
if idnum > 300 then output dept;
```

```
run;
```
A. There is no error in the program. It will compile, execute, and produce the expected result.
B. SAS will detect a semantic error, but will continue processing the program. SAS will then send a warning to the log explaining the action taken.
C. SAS will detect the error and stop processing the program.
D. SAS will detect a syntax error, correct the problem, and send a warning to the log.

14. How would you correct the situation in the previous problem?
A. Add a LIBNAME statement to the beginning of the program.
B. Delete the SET statement.
C. There is no problem to be corrected.
D. Change the name of the dataset in the output statement to 'dpart'.

15. When SAS detects an execution–time error, what does it usually do?
A. It generates an error message and continues processing the program.
B. It generates a warning and a note, and continues to process the program.
C. It sends an error message to the log beginning with the word ERROR and stops processing the program.
D. It sends an error message to the log, sets _ERROR_ = 1, and stops processing the program.

16. When does an execution–time error take place?
A. When a data value is not appropriate for the program written
B. When program statements do not conform to the rules of the SAS language
C. When SAS applies compiled programs to data values
D. When SAS statements are correct, but the elements are not valid for that usage

17. An illegal argument to a function produces
A. A semantic error
B. A data error
C. A syntax error
D. An execution-time error

18. If there is division by zero in a program, what type of error will it produce?
A. Syntax
B. Data
C. Execution-time
D. Semantic

19. If you encounter the condition "not enough memory" or "disk is full", what kind of error will it produce?
A. Execution–time error.
B. Data error.
C. Semantic error.
D. No error will be produced.

20. If the following program is executed, an execution-time error will be produced.
```
Data a;
Input name $ salary index;
bonus = salary / index;
datalines;
brendel 50000 10
hicks 65000 20
hill 71000 0
brown 54000 12
;
run;
```

You can solve the problem by
A. Adding the following statement: `if index ge 0 the bonus = salary / index;`
B. Adding the following statement: `if index gt 0 then bonus = salary / index;`
C. By removing the statement `dataline;`
D. By removing the INPUT statement

21. In the following program, the semicolon at the end of the TITLE statement is missing. If you run this program, what kind of error will it produce, if any?
A. A syntax error
B. A semantic error
C. An execution-time error
D. No error will be produced; only a warning message will be issued.

22. If you run the following program, an execution–time error will be produced.
```
Data empnum;
Array y(*) y1 - y3;
Input n empno;
If empno > 0 then y(n) = empno;
Datalines;
1 2
3 4
5 6
;
run;
```

You can avoid this problem by
A. Changing the statement: `array y(*) y1 - y3;` to `array y1 - y5;`
B. Changing the statement: `array y(*) y1 - y3 ;` to `array y(*) y1- y2;`
C. Deleting the data statement
D. Deleting the conditional statement

23. Data error is detected by SAS during the

A. Compilation of the program
B. Execution of the program
C. Data error is rarely detected by SAS. You notice it when you check the output data and see discrepancies in output values.
D. This kind of error can be detected during either compilation or execution of the program depending on your environment

24. With data error
    A. Something is wrong with program statements.
    B. Something is wrong with data values.
    C. Program statements do not comply with SAS rules.
    D. Program statements are correct but are not suitable for data at hand.

25. In the following program, what causes the error?

```
Data abc;
Input name $ salary;
Datallines;
Valk 55000
Louder 61000
Cool $65000
Cook12 76000;
run;
```

    A. The input statement.
    B. The variable `salary` is numeric, while one of the data values is character.
    C. One of the names has numric values.
    D. When you run this program, no error will be produced.

26. When you run the following program, you will get an error. How would you solve the problem?

```
Data empdate;
Input name $ bdate mmddyy10.;
Datalines;
Jones 020298
Barns 083299
Barock 090902
;
run;
```

    A. In the first line of data, change the value of year to 1998.
    B. Change the informat of the variable `bdate` to `mmddyy8`.
    C. Change the value of 02 to 2002.
    D. Change the value of 32 to a number that is at most 31.

27. When do we have a logic error in a program?
    A. When a SAS program is not appropriate for a data value
    B. When a SAS program compiles correctly but fails to execute
    C. When program statements do not conform to the rules of SAS language

D. When a program compiles and executes with no problem but the result in the output is not what it should be

28. Which one of the following will produce a logic error?
   A. The number of months in a year is entered as 13.
   B. A semicolon is omitted at the end of input statement.
   C. There are unmatched quotation marks in the program.
   D. A keyword is misspelled.

29. If you fail to mention a dataset for your SAS program, what type of error will you most likely create?
   A. Semantic
   B. Syntax
   C. Data
   D. Logic

30. Which one of the following is used to find logic errors?
   A. SAS DEBUGGER
   B. PROC step DEBUGGER
   C. DATA step DEBUGGER
   D. PUT statement DEBUGGER

31. Which one of the following is used to find a logic error?
   A. A SET statement
   B. A DEBUG statement
   C. A PROC statement
   D. A PUT statement.

Practice exam answers

1. B
2. C
3. B
4. D
5. A
6. A
7. B
8. C
9. D
10. B
11. C
12. C
13. C
14. D
15. B
16. C
17. D

18. C
19. A
20. B
21. C
22. A
23. B
24. B
25. B
26. D
27. D
28. A
29. D
30. C
31. D

Problems

In each of the following problems a program is run and the content of the SAS log is given. Read the program carefully and identify the source(s) of error(s).

1.
```
data a ;
input fname $ lname $ id;
dataines;
david edwards 1001
johnay jone 1002
barara cook 1003
;
run;
proc print data=a;
run;
```

Log:

```
39    data a ;
40      input fname $ lname $ id;
NOTE: SCL source line.
41    dataines;
      --------
      14
WARNING 14-169: Assuming the symbol DATALINES was misspelled as dataines.
NOTE: The data set WORK.A has 3 observations and 3 variables.
NOTE: DATA statement used:
      real time              0.05 seconds
45    ;
46    run;
47    proc print data=a;
48    run;
NOTE: There were 3 observations read from the data set WORK.A.
NOTE: PROCEDURE PRINT used:
      real time              0.05 seconds
```

2. Apart from finding the source for a syntax error, notice also that PROC PRINT identifies three lines of data to be printed. If there is (are) syntax error(s) in the program, then why are three lines of output printed?

```
data a ;
input fname $ lname $ id
datalines;
david edwards 1001
johnay jone 1002
barara cook 1003
;
run;
proc print data=a;
run;
```

Log:

```
69    data a
NOTE: SCL source line.
```

```
70     input fname $ lname $ id
                     _     _
                    22    22
                   _____  __
                    202   202
ERROR 22-322: Syntax error, expecting one of the following: a name, a
quoted string, (, /, ;,
               _DATA_, _LAST_, _NULL_.
ERROR 202-322: The option or parameter is not recognized and will be
ignored.
71     datalines;
NOTE: SCL source line.
72     david edwards 1001
       _____
        180
ERROR 180-322: Statement is not valid or it is used out of proper order.
73     johnay jone 1002
74     barara cook 1003
75     ;
76     run;
NOTE: The SAS System stopped processing this step because of errors.
WARNING: The data set WORK.A may be incomplete.  When this step was stopped
there were 0
          observations and 0 variables.
WARNING: Data set WORK.A was not replaced because this step was stopped.
WARNING: The data set WORK.INPUT may be incomplete.  When this step was
stopped there were 0
          observations and 0 variables.
WARNING: The data set WORK.FNAME may be incomplete.  When this step was
stopped there were 0
          observations and 0 variables.
WARNING: The data set WORK.LNAME may be incomplete.  When this step was
stopped there were 0
          observations and 0 variables.
WARNING: The data set WORK.ID may be incomplete.  When this step was
stopped there were 0
          observations and 0 variables.
WARNING: The data set WORK.DATALINES may be incomplete.  When this step was
stopped there were 0
          observations and 0 variables.
NOTE: DATA statement used:
      real time          0.27 seconds
77     proc print data=a;
78     run;
NOTE: There were 3 observations read from the data set WORK.A.
NOTE: PROCEDURE PRINT used:
      real time          0.00 seconds
```

3.  ```
    libname a 'c:\mydata';
    proc summary data=a.books mon;
    var cost;
    class author;
    output out=newbook;
    run;
    proc print data=newbook;
    run;
    ```

    ```
    Log:
    147  libname a 'c:\mydata';
    NOTE: Libref A was successfully assigned as follows:
          Engine:        V8
          Physical Name: c:\mydata
    NOTE: SCL source line.
    148  proc summary data=a.books mon;
    ```
    ```

```
                              ---
                              22
                              -
                              200
      ERROR 22-322: Syntax error, expecting one of the following: ;, (, ALPHA,
CHARTYPE, CLASSDATA,
                CLM, COMPLETETYPES, CSS, CV, DATA, DESCEND, DESCENDING,
DESCENDTYPES, EXCLNPWGT,
                EXCLNPWGTS, EXCLUSIVE, FW, IDMIN, KURTOSIS, LCLM, MAX,
MAXDEC, MEAN, MEDIAN, MIN,
                MISSING, N, NDEC, NMISS, NONOBS, NOPRINT, NOTRAP, NWAY,
ORDER, P1, P10, P25, P5,
                P50, P75, P90, P95, P99, PCTLDEF, PRINT, PRINTALL,
PRINTALLTYPES, PRINTIDS,
                PRINTIDVARS, PROBT, Q1, Q3, QMARKERS, QMETHOD, QNTLDEF,
QRANGE, RANGE, SKEWNESS,
                STDDEV, STDERR, SUM, SUMSIZE, SUMWGT, T, UCLM, USS, VAR,
VARDEF.
      ERROR 200-322: The symbol is not recognized and will be ignored.
      149  var cost;
      150  class author;
      151  output out=newbook;
      152  run;
      NOTE: The SAS System stopped processing this step because of errors.
      WARNING: The data set WORK.NEWBOOK may be incomplete.  When this step was
      stopped there were 0
              observations and 0 variables.
      WARNING: Data set WORK.NEWBOOK was not replaced because this step was
      stopped.
      NOTE: PROCEDURE SUMMARY used:
            real time              0.00 seconds
```

4.
```
proc summary data=b.books ;
var cost;
class author;
output out=newbook;
run;
```

```
Log:
169  proc summary data=b.books ;
ERROR: Libname B is not assigned.
170  var cost;
ERROR: No data set open to look up variables.
171  class author;
ERROR: No data set open to look up variables.
172  output out=newbook;
173  run;
NOTE: The SAS System stopped processing this step because of errors.
WARNING: The data set WORK.NEWBOOK may be incomplete.  When this step was
stopped there were 0
        observations and 0 variables.
WARNING: Data set WORK.NEWBOOK was not replaced because this step was
stopped.
NOTE: PROCEDURE SUMMARY used:
      real time              0.06 seco
```

5.
```
data empl;
array xx(*) ss1 - ss3;
xx=6;
datalines;
1 100
2 200
```

```
3 300
4 400
;
run;


Log:
176   data empl;
177   array xx(*) ss1 - ss3;
178   xx=6;
ERROR: Illegal reference to the array xx.
179   datalines;
NOTE: The SAS System stopped processing this step because of errors.
WARNING: The data set WORK.EMPL may be incomplete.  When this step was
stopped there were 0
        observations and 3 variables.
NOTE: DATA statement used:
      real time          0.38 seconds
```

6.  ```
    libname ab 'c\mydata';
    data newbooks book;
    set a.books;
    if cost  > 9.99 then output abc;
    run;


    Log:
    218   libname ab 'c\mydata';
    NOTE: Library AB does not exist.
    219   data newbooks;
    220   set a.books;
    NOTE: SCL source line.
    221   if cost  > 9.99 then output abc;
                                       ---
                                       455
    ERROR 455-185: Data set was not specified on the DATA statement.
    222   run;
    NOTE: The SAS System stopped processing this step because of errors.
    WARNING: The data set WORK.NEWBOOKS may be incomplete.  When this step was
    stopped there were 0
            observations and 7 variables.
    NOTE: DATA statement used:
          real time          0.05 seconds
    ```

7.  ```
    data clean;
    input dirt noparti;
    degcl = dirt / noparti;
    datalines;
    123 0.8
    324 0.89
    431 0.32
    443 0.0
    351 .21
    ;
    run;
    proc print data=clean;
    run;
    ```

```
Log:
228   data clean;
229   input dirt noparti;
230   degcl = dirt / noparti;
231   datalines;
NOTE: Division by zero detected at line 230 column 14.
RULE:        ----+----1----+----2----+----3----+----4----+----5----+----6----
+----7----+----8----+---
235        443 0.0
dirt=443 noparti=0 degcl=. _ERROR_=1 _N_=4
NOTE: Mathematical operations could not be performed at the following
places. The results of the
      operations have been set to missing values.
      Each place is given by: (Number of times) at (Line):(Column).
      1 at 230:14
NOTE: The data set WORK.CLEAN has 5 observations and 3 variables.
NOTE: DATA statement used:
      real time            0.04 seconds
237   ;
238   run;
239   proc print data=clean;
240   run;
NOTE: There were 5 observations read from the data set WORK.CLEAN.
NOTE: PROCEDURE PRINT used:
      real time            0.05 seconds
```

8.
```
data clean;
input dirt noparti;
title 'The Degree of Cleannes'
degcl = dirt / noparti;
datalines;
123 0.8
324 0.89
431 0.32
443 0.9
351 .21
;
run;
proc print data=clean;
run;
```

```
Log:

254   data clean;
255   input dirt noparti;
256   title 'The Degree of Cleannes'
257   degcl = dirt / noparti;
WARNING: The TITLE statement is ambiguous due to invalid options or
unquoted text.
258   datalines;
NOTE: The data set WORK.CLEAN has 5 observations and 2 variables.
NOTE: DATA statement used:
      real time            0.06 seconds
264   ;
265   run;
266   proc print data=clean;
267   run;
NOTE: There were 5 observations read from the data set WORK.CLEAN.
NOTE: PROCEDURE PRINT used:
      real time            0.00 seconds
```

9.  ```
    data arry;
    array y(*) y1 - y3;
    input num idnum;
    if idnum > 0 then y(num) = idnum;
    datalines;
    1 2
    3 4
    5 6
    ;
    Run;
    ```

    ```
    Log:
    68   data arry;
    269  array y(*) y1 - y3;
    270  input num idnum;
    271  if idnum > 0 then y(num) = idnum;
    272  datalines;
    ERROR: Array subscript out of range at line 271 column 19.
    RULE:        ----+----1----+----2----+----3----+----4----+----5----+----6----
    +----7----+----8----+---
    275       5 6
    y1=. y2=. y3=. num=5 idnum=6 _ERROR_=1 _N_=3
    NOTE: The SAS System stopped processing this step because of errors.
    WARNING: The data set WORK.ARRY may be incomplete.  When this step was
    stopped there were 2
             observations and 5 variables.
    NOTE: DATA statement used:
          real time               0.04 seconds
    ```

10. ```
    data hp;
    input fname $ lname $ bdate mmddyy10.;
    datalines;
    fred back 12121999
    bob wood 013380
    jane ross 08111998
    george dadoo 02041976
    ;
    run;
    proc print data=hp;
    run;
    ```

    ```
    Log:
    332  data hp;
    333  input fname $ lname $ bdate mmddyy10.;
    334  datalines;
    NOTE: Invalid data for bdate in line 336 10-19.
    RULE:        ----+----1----+----2----+----3----+----4----+----5----+----6----
    +----7----+----8----+---
    336        bob wood 01331980
    fname=bob lname=wood bdate=. _ERROR_=1 _N_=2
    NOTE: The data set WORK.HP has 4 observations and 3 variables.
    NOTE: DATA statement used:
          real time               0.05 seconds
    339  ;
    340  run;
    341  proc print data=hp;
    ```

```
342  run;
NOTE: There were 4 observations read from the data set WORK.HP.
NOTE: PROCEDURE PRINT used:
```

11.
```
data bloodpr;
input name $ age bloodp;
datalines;
davidson 23 80
jordan 35 92
hick 45 95
vonn 53 78
;
run;
proc print ;
run;
```

Log:

```
Obs     fname      lname        bdate
              1     fred       back      12/12/1999
              2     bob        wood      01/31/1980
              3     jane       ross      08/11/1998
              4     george     dadoo     02/04/1976
```

Problem solutions

1. The key word `datalines` is misspelled as `dataines`.
2. A semicolon is omitted from the first line. The reason for three lines of output is that SAS uses the latest dataset available to print.
3. The option `min` is misspelled `mon`.
4. The LIBNAME statement is omitted.
5. Line `xx = 5;` is the source of the problem.
6. The name of the output dataset `abc` is not mentioned in the DATA statement.
7. The source of the problem is division by zero. On line 4 of the data the value of the variable `noparti` is zero. To avoid the problem, enter the following line of code:
   `if noparti > 0 then degcl = dirt / noparti`
8. The semicolon at the end of the TITLE statement is left out.
9. You can avoid this problem by changing the line `y(*) y1 - y3;` to `array y1 - y5;`.
10. The number of days in a month is typed to be 33, while the maximum number of days in a month is 31.
11. Notice that the program has no error, but the output is the one from the last problem. The reason is that no dataset is given in the PROC PRINT, so SAS prints the last dataset available.

Index